# Beyond the Rainbow Cloud

### Jeannie H. Judd
plus channelling
### Geoff Hamilton

# www.capallbann.co.uk

# Beyond the Rainbow Cloud

©2002 Jeannie H. Judd

ISBN 186163 1464

Cover design by Paul Mason

Published by:

Capall Bann Publishing
Auton Farm
Milverton
Somerset
TA4 1NE

# Contents

This book is dedicated to Geoff with eternal love and appreciation for all the guidance, help and companionship generously given with amazing patience and endless good humour.

It was never my intention to profit personally in any way from the proceeds of this book. The value of this contact and all it brings means far more to me than any financial gain could possibly offer. However, I feel there should be further lasting benefit beyond the knowledge given. Therefore I plan to set up a fund to create a centre in Geoff's name. An advanced spiritual/psychic centre of excellence, to promote truth alongside uniting spirit and physical beings, working together in harmony and co-operation to benefit this planet and all species living on it. No such centre would be complete without gardens, and I intend these to be faithful recreations of the gardens Geoff has now in spirit. And all profits therefore will go towards this aim.

# Acknowledgements

I couldn't begin this without expressing my greatest thanks to Geoff, without whom there wouldn't have been a book at all. But much more than that, thank you for all you do for me, for all the knowledge, for all you teach me, for all you show me, for all the laughter and magic, for all the companionship, and for all the private moments that haven't gone into this book.

Enormous thanks too go to a special friend, Lesley, for sharing in part, my journey of discovery and awakening. For having the wisdom to see things I missed, and for interpreting where I couldn't. There were times when I think I may have given up without you.

My thanks too to Paul for the support. Writing a book such as this requires dedication and attention to detail, and a lot of time in physical silence supplied with regular cups of tea.

Thank you to all those who shared their own experiences with me. Your truth and honesty removes misconceptions and shows the unlimited reality of the dimensions around us.Too much has been hidden for too long. Let the light shine now.

I want to thank Julie Gale for her book *Soul Trek*. Geoff asked me to read this book as it would help me to understand a lot. It has become a valued friend I read again and again. The only book on this subject that makes complete sense to me from start to finish. I wouldn't hesitate to recommend it to anyone.

Our sincere thanks to publishers Capall Bann, and Julia Day. In these cynical and sceptical times it is wonderful to find those who recognise, support and encourage real values and truths, thus allowing those who seek, access to knowledge and information.

Finally, my heartfelt thanks to all the guides, helpers and angels who assisted in bringing about this contact and helped make it so strong. Thank you for all the protection down the years, and for keeping us safe now.

# Introduction

I am starting this book without knowing just where it will lead, or even, what will be written in it. All I am sure of is, it will be the story of a journey and personal experience of things not many have been privileged to have, at least while in physical form. I hope it may open up closed minds and create new avenues of reality which will birth a better world, eventually.

There are far more things around us than anyone has an explanation for. Some claim to, and many take the role of debunker, and inevitably they will rise up en masse to discredit my experiences. That isn't important and matters little to me because I KNOW deep within that all I have experienced happened. That is my knowledge and each debunker must find their own way. What does concern me is that these people are trotted out and presented as some kind of 'expert'. Then the danger is that they turn away those who are just finding their way into the light and that is the greatest wrong to be done to them. So to those who want to believe let me say just this, keep an open mind and remember, these 'experts' debunk simply because they have no experience of the very thing they are debunking. So how can they be 'expert' in something they have no knowledge of? Nor will they have while they so adamantly disbelieve. Sciences may have their uses, but not everything can be proven, not yet anyway.

This isn't just an account of my experiences, some of which are too special and personal to share, so must remain mine alone. Although this book tells of a remarkable and strong

Jeannie H. Judd

contact from beyond this physical world, an actual close and wonderful relationship even, what we are really attempting to demonstrate is that nothing is impossible now with a totally open mind. We are on the threshold of a New Age, an age of real enlightenment and surfacing of our true selves. Eventually, this will lead to a better world as we realise our own responsibility in everything. We will understand that whatever our reality is, good, bad or indifferent, we create it ourselves. Once we fully accept that very basic truth, we see there are no victims, no-one else we can blame for our lives, then we can set about doing things right for ourselves, those around us, and our world.

Greed, selfishness, sheer indifference to the needs of others and the needs of our Earth; all these have grown beyond reason for decades. People have lost their way and there has been little real guidance. There is purpose in this. For far too long we have been controlled by religions, governments, business interests, and the need to sustain an ever growing, chaotic population. Now we have been through a period of great uncertainty, fear, lack of security and little peace of mind. There have been no answers deliberately, forcing people to start thinking for themselves, seeking, rejecting the old orders which have prevented them from finding the truth by insisting this must be believed, or that, without anything genuine to back it up. Enormous changes in consciousness are emerging as we go into a new century. Much greater communication and co-operation will take place between worlds. The result will be a leap forward in human evolution which will not only benefit our world, but the entire Universe, and right back to The Source itself.

We are all spirit first and foremost. Our lifetimes on this physical world are brief sojourns to learn, experience, gain knowledge, and work through the law of cause and effect (karma). In that respect we would all gain by doing our very best always. Some lessons take a lot of learning and require several lifetimes to complete. It makes no difference if you believe this or not, the law is absolute and makes no exceptions. What you find and experience when you leave this world depends on how you live your physical lives. If you always do your best selflessly, there is nothing to fear, your experience will be joyful.

There is one key that opens all locks, a key which runs through everything and is the only thing we take with us from life to life. That key is LOVE. When we truly love, we have no wish to harm or damage. When we know we are truly loved, we are secure, can grow, progress, evolve. It is with love we create positively, and true love overcomes all things, heals all things. In this book we hope to explain different kinds of love, all of them valid, and how the New Age will see important changes in our earthly relationships. Changes that are necessary to harmonising life on this planet.

We all have free will, that is never violated, but sometimes this can lead us astray by stubbornly rejecting guidance and our own intuition, thus preventing what was intended from manifesting. When we have no flow or movement in our lives and seem to be stuck in situations not of our conscious choosing, it is probably because we have over-used our free will and taken a wrong turning. We all do it, it is part of human nature and when so much is veiled from us, we often struggle on as best we can, but making mistakes is part of the learning. Maybe after reading this book, you will be more alert to those clues and other things which are always available to us and if it helps others achieve the kind of life they want and deserve, then we will have done well.

My contact with Geoff has been a tremendous voyage of discovery. He has helped me overcome my 'amnesia', something we all suffer as we go into each physical life, to surface memories of other lifetimes and retain memories of our work and other experiences together now, including two brief but special times when our paths crossed in this lifetime. Only recently I realised, those times happened when I was experiencing great traumas in my young life. And the time when he made contact in 1996, events in my life had created the greatest trauma, a bleak, black time from which I could see no respite, no hope. I have no doubt there is something in that which goes far beyond physical understanding. Some Divine energy that works for us, bringing such things about through the threads of continuance. I cannot fully express in words, my gratitude for all he has done for me. Only his strength of character, personality and perseverance enabled him to get through to me at all. It was the darkest time of my life and one where I'd lapsed into absolute denial. I call that time the 'dark night of my soul' and without doubt, his timely intervention saved me from an awful fate. And as our contact has grown and progressed I have gained in strength and confidence in ways I once wouldn't have thought possible. Such things inevitably change you and I knew from early on, nothing would ever be the same again. Although our contact is the strongest I have ever known, and the most amazing happening of all the amazing events of my life, it is not unique. I correspond with others experiencing similarly, and am always pleased to expand this circle. And I stress, such contacts are available to all who seek and open their minds by suspending the eons of restrictive and limiting beliefs and doctrines.

During the course of this contact, friends and acquaintances who know of it often ask questions of Geoff. His answers produce gems of knowledge which are so well received, it was eventually suggested they should be shared with a wider audience, and so the idea of this book was born. It has grown into a comprehensive picture of life in that other dimension we will all find ourselves in one day, and of relative purposes of our physical lives. Some of this will no doubt be surprising, perhaps even come as a shock to some, but Geoff's intention always, is to bring through truth in an entertaining and

Jeannie's home from where she and her partner Paul run the P.A.W.S. animal sanctuary

enjoyable way. It is also his wish to demonstrate that he does indeed live on. I only realised the extent of this when a friend said she so often speaks of Geoff and things he has said, it keeps his presence here, actually making him more real now than when his programmes are repeated on television.That really expresses truly the reality of our etheric being, our true selves, and I feel a sense of awe in having a part to play in the understanding of that.

This book then, will hopefully give inspiration that leads to the finding of a better way to experience earthly incarnations through harmonious rapport with our friends and guides in Spirit. A new way of life and living which benefits all souls, and the worlds we live in.

# Geoff's Foreword

It is a great delight for me to be able to work on this project. If nothing else, I hope it makes many pause in their busy lives and consider if what we have to impart has meaning for them. Better still if some have an inner knowing that this is all correct. It wouldn't be possible to reach everyone and many have to find their own pathway to knowledge and truth. All I can ask is for you to seek. All I can do is speak my truth from my vantage point. Whether you believe all you read here is your choice, nobody will attempt to force you. But if our words make you open your minds just a little, seek further, and leave you with a glimmer of hope that wasn't there before, we will have achieved all we set out to do. We will have sown those seeds which with careful nurturing, can grow into a whole new way of living, a new dawn of contentment and hope.

In many ways I am still a new boy here but that is no bad thing because it means I can still relate closely to physical life. I have chosen to remain close to earth; earth-bound some describe it somewhat inaccurately; for several reasons, not least to be able to communicate something of this 'other' world I now exist in. My hope is to reach many people, to give an understanding of continuance. A light to cast aside the fear of something that has perplexed for centuries. And a glimmer of perception on what physical life is all about. Knowledge is liberating and to be part of bringing a measure of that back, is a privilege, and thanks for a fairly fortunate life this time around.

There may well be some information included in this book, of a controversial nature. I make no apologies or excuses for this. So much has been hidden and distorted for too long. I am not afraid of controversy and in the interests of accuracy, image matters little. If you have read other books about life in these realms, you will no doubt find elements of information that differs, even contradicts in some cases. The reason for this is that we are all at different levels and stages of progress. There are many, many dimensions and some offer a quite different way of life to the one I am now living.

The important thing to remember is not that some accounts are wrong necessarily, but that we are all individuals with varying beliefs and aspirations, and it is this factor that results in the seeming contradictions. Rather than dismiss them all, accept what feels comfortable to you and reject anything that makes you uneasy, in which case, the latter will not be your personal experience at this stage. But some gems will remain to give you inspiration for further searching. Few books of this nature will find total universal agreement and actually, that is how it should be.We don't have all the answers, but evolvement is progressive and things are speeding up generally. New information is necessary because many aspects have changed, and many more will do so in the next few years, leading to greater understanding, awareness and enlightenment, about life and all beyond that.

I have nothing but praise for my partner and co-worker in this project. My thanks to her for giving me this opportunity. It is entirely due to the longstanding link and bond between us that such excellent contact is possible. We are pioneers of sorts, and that suits me fine. One day, such contacts and communications will be completely normal occurrences and the physical limitations blocking so much of this 'other' world, will be history. Meanwhile, it is up to those such as us to lead the way and give reasons why we should examine the way we all live and see if we can do it better. In many areas we have been getting it wrong for a very long time and bear in mind the only ones that will hurt ultimately, is ourselves.

This book is very much a joint effort which I hope will give enjoyment and food for thought, if it completely opens even a few hearts and minds, then I will be well satisfied. We are not aiming at total conversion - new ideas need assimilating carefully. This really is the weaving of a tale of two lives, lived for the most part separate, yet intrinsically linked throughout nonetheless. In the telling of this, strands of knowledge interweave to give a picture of life beyond the physical dimension and of other matters. This is not a work of fiction, but of truths long hidden, long buried; from ourselves as much as anyone else. Thankfully, no longer so. The truths in these pages are not unique to us. They are truths and experiences available to each and every one of you. All you need to access the magic is an open mind, and a limitless belief that refuses to accept anything as impossible.

Inevitably there will be those who insist this communication cannot be coming from me. All I will say to that is fine, believe as you will, it is your choice. But I would ask you to bear in mind there has to be a difference in the way I communicate now. I can no longer stand up and speak physically and have to rely on the skill of my psychic friend. This accounts for odd foibles, but also, now free from physical limitations, I have greater awareness which allows me to explore possibilities I could never have once dreamed of. We remain the personality and form we were in life but have the advantage of access to knowledge of previous lives and other things. Since being in this dimension I have learned a tremendous lot, things which I would most likely have dismissed as rubbish while incarnate. This expands us considerably and makes it difficult sometimes for some still restricted by the physical, to relate to. Hopefully this aspect will become clearer through these pages. It is worth remembering too, while on Earth in physical form, however close we may be to others, however well we think we know another person, there is always a part of ourselves we hold back and never share. This has to be and it links deep within to our subconscious knowledge that physical life is only temporary, illusionary, and not the true reality. Again, I will attempt to present a clearer understanding of this because it makes sense of that which appears inexplicable.

During this past lifetime, I think I was rather lucky to have the kind of life that kept me content, doing what I enjoyed most and even better, earning a living at it. This project therefore is an attempt to give something back, my way of offering a bit of light on subjects which may seem way off my usual theme, but nonetheless, affect each and every one of us. However, as you will also discover here, I am still doing all the things that keep me happy, that give me great joy, and I plan to go on doing so for a good long while yet.

G.H.

# Chapter One

# In The Beginning

I have always been psychic. I gave it no name as a child, but accepted naturally the beings around me. Fortunately my Mother had some psychic experiences herself and my 'abilities' were not ridiculed or squashed. Not that they were actively encouraged either, merely accepted. My unseen 'companions' were part of my life and I never felt alone even though my many times of illness kept me segregated from physical companions. But spirit companionship was always there and on no occasion did it ever scare me. I have never been afraid of them, or of death, of which I seemed to have a deep inner instinctive understanding always.

Most of my unseen 'friends' were not other children but adult spirits. I was very well protected throughout childhood, wayward teens, and a violent first marriage. I have no doubts that without this protection I would not have survived any, or all, these phases in my life. However, until now, I never questioned why I should be so protected. It is only since conscious contact with Geoff that I have gained understanding, and knowledge of a mission and mutual work during unconscious sleep time, requiring such complete protection.

One of the most amazing examples of this protection came when I was ten years old. On a regular visit to an aunt living in remote countryside, bored with adult conversation, I went to call on a friend living further up the village. It was lunchtime but her Mother said I could wait in the garden for her. This was a big garden and on one side was a play area which included a swing. I chose this to pass the time as I waited. Absorbed in swinging I pushed it higher and higher, enjoying the far views. Recklessly I attempted to swing even higher still and the inevitable happened - this was an old fashioned, heavy wooden swing on chains, hung from a tubular metal frame. I swung up above the middle bar of this and it went right over the top! By all accounts I should have crashed onto the concrete below, probably hit at force by the returning swing, and crippled or worse. However, there was a moment of blackness as I parted company with the swing and the next thing I knew, I was lying in a vegetable patch some distance away and around a corner. I was shaken but totally unhurt, not even a scratch! I scrambled up scared someone from the house may have seen me and I would be in trouble. Nobody appeared and the vegetable patch which had cushioned me, was completely undamaged. The swing, who's chains should still have been across the centre bar, was returned to its normal position. This was perhaps the greatest, but only one of many such 'happenings' throughout my life, including almost being abducted by an undoubtedly perverted couple when I was seven who offered me chocolate to go with them and be 'photographed for a magazine'. I almost did so, then a voice told me to go and ask my Mother first. It was a most insistent voice that gave no leeway for argument. The couple said they would come back later when I had my Mother's agreement, I never saw them again of course.

Thoughts of any kind of purpose never occurred to me. This aspect aside, my life has not been easy. It has been one of constant struggle really, starting with the absence of my father from four months before I was born. This event coloured most of my life. I was never told much about him and as a result, I grew up lacking much feeling of identity, roots, and never feeling really part of a family. My birth came at the end of the war, not an easy time for anyone but in those days before introduction of the welfare state, there was no option but for my Mother to work, leaving me to be cared for by her aunt, my great-aunt, with whom we then lived. During much of my school days, she did two part time evening jobs as well as a full time day job. This increased the feelings of lacking a real family environment. Perhaps it was this background that has always given me a sense of other worlds and something beyond the physical reality around me.

It was a fairly solitary childhood in terms of physical companions of my own age. But my unseen 'friends' were always there to care and comfort, and I suspect, teach too. I had almost every childhood ailment going, some of them twice like Scarlet Fever. My great-aunt, bless her, without realising the effect on a child's mind, suggested it might have been better if I'd never been born in the circumstances, and I believe I did my best to propel myself out of this world again as quickly as possible. Having survived childhood with enormous help, my guardian angel never lacked work, I plunged into wayward teenage years, diving into every risky situation I could find! I came through completely unscathed somehow, not without divine intervention for sure, only to rush into a marriage which tested every area of marital disaster - violence; physical and verbal, excessive gambling and infidelity! It could only have been spiritual protection that got me through that, eighteen years of it, because I was determined my son would reach maturity with both a mother and father, and not part of a single parent family as I had been. I emerged from this time with all my values shaken to the core but I made the right decision for once. I couldn't wish for my son to have turned out any better. He has been very supportive, and is now well on the way to achieving his ambitions in professional photography, specialising in landscapes taken all around the world during his extensive travels.

It was during this marriage that I began to seriously follow a spiritual pathway, seeking out truth, sitting in a development circle and practising healing, particularly of animals. I have had a special affinity with animals and nature all my life. This aspect helped me overcome some of the blackest periods of despair, losing myself in the amazing beauty to be found in the simplest things; the unconditional love and trust in a pet's eyes; sunlight filtering through to pattern a woodland path; the iridescent sheen on a tiny insect; a rainbow. I can never understand how some look at these, and more, and not believe in continuance. How very sad to go through life, whatever that life brings, feeling that at the end of it, that is it. Even more sad, those with that belief block themselves from evidence and wonderful experiences, because of holding onto that restrictive belief.

Ever since my teens I have described my feelings about it all, as having a foot in each world. Recently I discovered this is how Shaman describe themselves although I don't actually place myself in any conventional category. This is simply the way I saw it, and all the inexplicable things that have happened to me throughout the years. Things like spontaneous out of the body experiences which I have had from time to time, and amazing happenings cropping up 'out of the blue'. All of it, I can see now, preparing me in every way for what was to come.

Following my divorce I changed my life completely and with a new partner in tow, decided to devote myself to animals and nature. Gradually the pain of previous years faded. There was little time for spiritual matters with a shop to run and many animals to care for. Even less when we decided to move to the country and start a sanctuary for all creatures, which eventually became a registered charity. However, nothing went smoothly during this entire period, we lost all our money and ended up in temporary housing where we became totally stuck. All efforts to recover our losses, caused by an inept

Some of the goats at the P.A.W.S. sanctuary.
From left to right: Tassie, Beattie (mum) and Twiglet

Possum

solicitor, failed, and confused by no movement or flow in life for several years, I began to turn against the spiritual side which had protected and sustained me for so long. By 1996 I was at my lowest, blackest point, totally in denial, totally depressed, and on a very slippery slope which would probably have led to suicide and not very far off either.

I have called this period my 'dark night of the soul'. I shut down completely on spirit and none could reach me. I think sometimes it is necessary to go through such times of trial, when we have taken wrong turnings and lost our way. When nothing flows, it is a sure sign we have gone wrong some- where, but until we can see it for ourselves, nothing can change. Before this ten year period I'd had tremendous flow in my life. Wonderful things happened 'out of the blue' without me even trying. My love of animals led to me being very involved with fancy rats and the society of that name. I not only enjoyed the social aspect of showing, breeding, judging, but also had many opportunities through this, to demonstrate the appeal of these intelligent creatures publicly, on radio and TV, something I found immensely satisfying. I had a wide circle of friends, acquaintances, and was in demand both here and abroad, for my gained experience and expertise covering the entire field of fancy rats and their care. I wrote a regular column for a specialist journal too, and had no reason to think anything other than life was truly opening up for me all round. Yet from 1986 it all ground to a complete halt.

When we come into physical life there are things we pre- arrange, things we agree to do, but that aside, we create the reality of our lives as we go along. The purposes agreed for any life, we hold at subconscious level, attracting as we go along, the necessary requirements to fulfil these. Such is the nature of free will, we sometimes stray from the route we set out to follow, and when this happens, we are given clues and opportunities to get back on course. But there is nobody to force us in any way, that would be a violation of our own will.

Our lives are not predestined therefore, if they were, we would be little more than puppets. The problems arise when our stubbornness makes us ignore the clues we are given, the guidance that is always available, and we go our own way, which, if the wrong way, leads to a limbo-like existence which will go on until we learn and get back on track.This isn't something outside of our control. We do it ourselves, knowing at some inner level we have gone wrong somewhere. We block ourselves, knowing we have to fulfil our inbuilt purposes for this lifetime.The more important that purpose, the more blocked we become when going astray.

It is easy to dismiss these things and sceptics will eagerly do so, but where lives are extremely hard and burdened, to endure it with the thought it is the only one, must make that lifetime even worse to bear. And to think that way makes little sense of life at all.What is the point of it all if you are just born, live and then die, once only? It might be acceptable if your whole life is wonderful, no pain, no suffering, and everything going your way from start to finish. Few lives are like that, and if they are, it will be for two reasons; one, it has been earned by a previous lifetime of total sacrifice; two, it will be a learning experience to see how you handle it and behave towards others.

Although during my 'dark' time I too denied all this, things I have known since very young - I don't mean by that, things I have been indoctrinated with, but things I knew inside beyond any doubt - there was still protection going on for me, and my unseen friends tried many ways to reach me again, to draw me back onto the spiritual pathway I had adamantly rejected. All to no avail until something happened that shook me so completely, to soul level, and yet at that time, totally inexplicably - Geoff Hamilton died on August 4th, 1996.

I have had many experiences of death throughout my life and always taken them in my stride, with understanding. Why then did this death affect me so much? Like many others very keen on gardening, I was inspired by Geoff. In fact I regarded him as my mentor, learning all I knew from him, so much so, that when faced with a job I was unsure about, I would just think of him and what to do, and immediately the answer was right there in my mind. It never failed. I wasn't even aware then that our paths had crossed twice in this lifetime, when I was very young, and it never occurred to me to question just why Geoff was always so familiar. It was just that he had always been there, and now he had gone.

I still recall that day vividly. A warm gentle day. In early evening I met my neighbour, another keen gardener whom I had obviously often quoted Geoff to. She greeted me with, had I heard the news, that my friend had died? That was all she said but I knew immediately. I went icy cold, as if the sun had suddenly been switched off, and something close to panic gripped me. This reaction was spontaneous and I had to fight to achieve control as I felt myself on the point of blacking out. I remember thinking and saying, whatever will I do now? And for the very first time ever in my life, I felt utterly alone.

In the days that followed my blackness and depression deepened so I still didn't question why I had reacted as I did. I doubt my thinking was coherent in any case as my mind seemed to go round and round in confused circles. My life, which had been stuck for so long, now seemed pointless. By the end of August I was closer to wanting it all to end than ever before. I had no way of describing what I was feeling but knew somehow my life had changed completely, and that it would never be the same ever again. Right at my lowest ebb I had an unexpected visit from an old friend whom I hadn't seen for many years. I have no doubts this 'out of the blue' event was arranged in spirit because this visit gave me a boost, lifted me sufficiently out of that blackness just long enough. A few days after this, Geoff contacted me for the first time.

24

# Chapter Two

# Contact And Communication

It was about six weeks after he died, in September, when Geoff first made contact and got through to me. It can't have been easy as I was completely closed down to any psychic experience. Such was the blackness surrounding me, Geoff described it as a 'cloak of depression which I'd wrapped tightly around me', that his first attempt failed. He decided therefore, to try in the way that we had been doing rescue work for years, during sleep state.

So the first contact was like a dream, yet more lucid and unforgettable than any dream could be, with full awareness and all senses registering everything. In the morning I remembered every moment of it and even now, almost two years later, the evocative call of seagulls transports me right back to that first contact with my memory vividly intact. And it has never faded.

It began in a museum, but no museum on this world as this one showed the true history of mankind. There were four of us, Geoff enlisted two others who had previously worked with us during sleep state, to help him get through. There was no strangeness as it was just like the harmony while working, even though apparently we hadn't undertaken any of that for over a year. (I will leave Geoff to describe this work as he now has complete access to remembering it all. I have surfaced

**25**

some memories and of course, consciously recall the work we are doing now, but most of it from that time, is still hidden from me).

Leaving the museum we walked along a sea front. It was day and there were several other people walking about. A low wall separated the promenade from the beach. We sat on this and our two companions found deckchairs, placing them opposite. We all enjoyed ourselves, talking laughing, and reminiscing. I could smell the sea air, hear the sound of the waves behind us, and the poignant call of the gulls overhead. It was at this moment I realised this was not Earth but an astral world and very soon, Geoff would have to go back again, into the spirit realms. I began crying, softly, as I didn't want the others to know, but Geoff realised and understood. He didn't hesitate for an instant but put his arms around me and said quietly, "It's all right. Really, everything is all right. I will be back."

In the morning these words echoed through my head.But I didn't realise then it was anything more than a dream, and although it didn't fade, as the days passed I thought of it as just a pleasant, but ordinary experience.Then exactly eight days later, it happened again.

Again it was a seaside area on an astral world, whether the same one or another, I don't know. There are billions of realms, or more accurately, levels of vibration and light, from our own Earth, the densest, to the highest, finest vibrations. These astral worlds fall somewhere between our world, and the etheric/spirit realms, vibrationally not as dense as Earth, but more so than the lower spirit realms. This is in a dimensional way since all worlds exist in the same space, it is only the dimension that alters according to the vibrational level we attain. The astral realms all have a purpose and some, such as these, provide a meeting place for us and our friends in spirit, for a vast variety of reasons. This time Geoff got through without needing the help of our comrades.We visited what at first glance, appeared like an amusement arcade. But these machines gave out gems of wisdom for those earnestly seeking, and those gems were greeted with great joy by the recipients. We left the building and walked along a path that climbed to the top of a high cliff. Far below, the sea gently brushed the shore and once more, seagulls called their melancholy cry. At the highest point of the cliff, we sat on the grass, intensely green, soft and thick, dotted with daisies and other wild flowers. It was incredibly peaceful with all the appearance of a perfect summer's day. We talked, joked, and then just sat enjoying the atmosphere and all around us. I was very relaxed and lay back closing my eyes, until I felt my nose being tickled by a piece of grass! At that moment, I knew intuitively the time was approaching when Geoff would again have to go back, and I must also return to my own dimension. I didn't cry but he sensed my sudden sadness and said very emphatically, "I haven't left you!" Again on waking this entire 'dream' remained vivid in my memory and has never faded.

Following the second 'dream' I wondered if they would continue and what it all meant. Still depressed I didn't once question why they were happening even though there was a quality about them that suggested far more than it appeared on the surface. Even so, they felt completely comfortable and quite normal, but as the days passed I began to doubt there would be another and put them down to 'coincidence'. Then another eight days later, there was a third.

The third 'dream' was in a different setting, a woodland, but on one side of this, a little stream bubbled its way down a slight slope, over rocks. A path meandered up through the tall trees and sunlight filtered through these to cast patterns along it. Beside the stream, a fallen tree lay undisturbed and here we sat to talk. Geoff described this place as, "possibly the last stronghold of natural grown broad-leafed limes". I felt from that, this beautiful place could actually be on Earth, but I wasn't certain.

Water seems important to communication with those in spirit. It creates a link, a flow, maybe because our dense physical bodies are mainly water. Maybe because water mirrors the fluidity and freedom of spirit. Watching the sparkling flow of this stream, it almost seemed hypnotic and very calming. On this occasion Geoff was more serious, explaining that it was still early days and these 'excursions' took a lot of energy which needed replenishing afterwards. We assume once in spirit, all things are known automatically, and once the physical body is shed, all things become easy. Geoff put me right on that informing me many things have to be learned and practised, just as here, and wouldn't it be rather boring otherwise! He was still adjusting and it would be easier therefore if I would be prepared to meditate, thus raising my own vibrations, concentrating on him, and then we could be in daily contact if I wished. I agreed but with reservations. It was many years since I last meditated regularly and I had serious doubts it would be successful. However, I intended to have a go as he had made such efforts to reach me, and I began, somewhat apprehensively, the next day.

That first meditation was simple but effective. I sat for quite a while trying to picture Geoff but I found it impossible to do so. I thought I might let him down and didn't want to do that, so instead, I concentrated on his name. Immediately he was there and I could see him clearly. He thanked me for trusting him enough to do this, and then explained what would happen this first time. There would be a column of light which we needed to stand in. This would attune our vibrations, uplifting mine at the same time, and this would make future meditations much easier as the link grew stronger. This happened as he said, and I was aware of great energy in this light, so strong that I actually felt a little wobbly and he said I should sit for a while afterwards, until the light-headedness went. As the light disappeared, Geoff thanked me again and asked if I would sit daily in meditation. I agreed to do so. It felt as if it had just been a few minutes but when I opened my eyes, exactly twenty minutes had passed and this time period marked all of our early meditation sessions.

It was a while after this that I learned that column of light had also cleared away a lot of the negativity clinging to me. When we are depressed, we attract negative elements which gather around us, drawn by our state of mind. This becomes a spiralling process as we sink lower into depression thus attracting even more negative elements, and the deeper we sink, the harder it is to climb back out of it. I discovered following that first meditation, I had a sense of joy, something which had been missing for a very long time, and looking back now, I don't think it is putting it too strongly to say, in finding me and getting through to me when he did, Geoff actually saved me, gently coaxing me back from the brink of complete disaster, so negative was the path I was then following.

We talked a lot during those early meditations. It was a slow awakening, and we were both still adjusting in our own ways. If my state hadn't been so dire, maybe he would have taken more time to settle there before attempting any contact. However, I soon found out just how resourceful he was, determined to investigate as many ways of communicating as possible. In October, he asked me to have a go at automatic writing! This is something I have never attempted and had little idea how to go about it. I bought a large drawing block and felt tipped pen. On Geoff's instruction I sat with eyes closed, pen held lightly over the paper, then switch off myself, allowing whatever might happen, to happen. We succeeded in a fashion, but I had to dicipher what was written each time. Sometimes this was easier than other times, usually when I asked him to slow down and please write a bit neater! We still have a weekly session of automatic writing, more for fun than anything else as we switched to using the word processor for a better way of covering more information.

Perhaps I should explain how this works and how Geoff is writing his sections of this book. I do not go into trance but slightly distance myself. This gives the sort of feeling we get just before sleep, a sort of drifting where you are only vaguely aware of what is going on around you. I am not sure where I am, it seems as if I am somehow beside myself, yet at the same time, still conscious. Geoff is able to take over but also, I hear the words in my head, like dictation. During these sessions, I don't feel my hands, I lose awareness of them as if they are numb. These sensations become less obvious as we have done more and more writing this way. Although I hear the words, they go immediately so that when I read back the pieces he has written, they are quite new to me, and usually most informative. This is necessary, otherwise my logical conscious mind would interfere, assessing what Geoff had written and attempting to alter it to fit the boundaries of what most people could accept and understand. This is not what Geoff wants.We are approaching a time where expanding our minds beyond restrictive beliefs is essential. Before starting on the book, Geoff produced a variety of short pieces giving information on many subjects to friends of mine, and by request from others, and these have been well received. We are including some of these in a later chapter.

Once the regular meditations were established and had been in practise almost a month, Geoff began to develop other ways of psychic and telepathic contact. He put songs in my head, and these would keep on persistently until I realised and recognised the message in them. As soon as I did so, they vanished and I had to struggle to recall them, particularly some that were not familiar to me. I quickly learned to keep a diary and note everything down straight away. Geoff also dictated a couple of pieces of poetry to me. These were quite beautiful, lines he had composed himself, but they didn't continue. He explained later writing 'proper' poetry wasn't really his thing, but at the time, it seemed the best way to get ideas across to me, and keep me interested!

Music provided a good link in those early days too. One day, looking around a shop selling new age items, I was drawn to and strongly impressed to buy a tape called 'Between Two Worlds'. The music on this is very relaxing and spiritual, and as well as aiding contact then, it also helped me over a panic attack during a power cut one evening. On my own in complete darkness and being attacked by negative thoughts, I suddenly heard Geoff telling me to play the tape on my personal stereo and this relaxed me enough for him to reassure me, something he had been trying to do for some time but I hadn't been aware of him in my panic. One of the pieces on this tape created a special link for us. It has a recording of seagulls in part of it.

It wasn't all sweetness and light though. For quite a while I was very difficult, a hangover from my dark days. I questioned constantly and was extremely sceptical, demanding frequent proofs, which I have to admit, he always provided. I was also often stroppy and stubborn, the latter being one of my challenges during this lifetime, and as a result, I had some formidable lectures from Geoff. During these, I felt like a small naughty child being told off, but afterwards, when I calmed down, I realised he was always right and scrupulously fair. One in particular was quite harrowing. It was a Sunday and I was being completely negative and demanding. For all the ways Geoff has succeeded communication-wise, he adamantly refuses to 'perform' on demand, and quite expressively says he has no intention of providing any little mediocre items of proof which any basic medium could come up with for anyone! This particular afternoon I'd foolishly expected something of him and worked myself up into quite a state when he refused. He left me to it for a while, but at the height of my rage, his voice cut in sharply, stopping me in my tracks. He went on for ages leaving me in no doubt of my mistake, and it worked. By the time he finished my anger had withered, and all I could do was apologise. Usually these incidents were never mentioned again, but after this one, he said he hadn't wanted to be so severe, or enjoyed it, but he could see me fast sinking back into self-destruct mode and had to do something fast. I could then accept it was fully justified.

It is now a very long time since I last needed to be lectured so I must have learned something. There is nobody else I would take that from, only the respect and trust I have always had in Geoff made me listen and understand it was only to help me. I did find it quite amusing that whenever he launched into a lecture he would appear to me very much as he was not long before leaving this world, whereas usually now, he has taken off at least twelve years, is full of energy and life, and always an inspiration of enthusiasm. Although we remain as the person we were in our last lifetime, we do revert to a time of that life when we felt at our best. Geoff explained this as the reason why, however old we get, we still feel young inside because our etheric/spirit bodies stop maturing at that ideal age. I once humourously suggested that when giving me a lecture, perhaps he felt the need to appear that bit older and with more authority. I couldn't repeat his reply to that!

It may sound as if I am a neurotic sort of person but this isn't so. I am actually usually fairly calm and able to cope adequately with all kinds of traumas. But that time was a culmination of frustrations, and it took a month or so for me to fully emerge from the depression that had haunted me for several years due to the sheer lack of movement in my life. Now I am rarely roused to temper and even when difficulties arise, I have total trust in Geoff and discuss everything with him. There is no subject or anything that is taboo, and frequently, our conversations and contact is full of laughter. We have a very similar sense of humour and he often teases me until I cannot speak for laughing, which usually starts him off too. It can be awkward sometimes. It is so natural now for me to be in conversation with Geoff, I forget other people probably cannot see or hear him, and I have received some very odd looks at times. Something which causes him much merriment, and me much embarrassment.

Those first few months I felt very insecure whenever Geoff went back to his own dimension. He always said if I needed him, I must call and he would be with me immediately. Although reluctant to disturb him, there were one or two occasions when I did so. He never once let me down or showed any sign of impatience even if the reason seemed trivial. My main worry whenever he stepped back was that he might not return and I would lose him again. Eventually I spoke of this fear. Geoff finding me, getting through to me when he did, totally changed my life around in ways I could never have imagined. I was afraid he would vanish one day and leave a void I could never hope to fill. He reassured me then and several times since, with a promise he will never leave me again. And I have come to understand since, Geoff never gives a firm promise on anything he is uncertain about.

Geoff took the lead right from the start and guided me through every stage. This was necessary given the state I was in, plus he now has much wider perspective and awareness on many things. I did however lay down one ground rule, I banned him from the bathroom! It didn't take very long before Geoff was able to contact me psychically and I became aware of his presence frequently at other times, outside of our regular meditation sessions, both indoors and outside.This isn't a problem to me at all, and I always welcome his company - except in the bathroom. He accepted and respected it but not very graciously, suggesting I was shutting him out which wasn't so. I just needed one room to maintain some dignity and privacy. However, he still gets his own way to some extent and although I am never actually aware of him in the bathroom, he creates a variety of phenomena almost every time I am in there! He also once informed me that even though he wasn't allowed in there, if necessary he could still talk to me because telepathy didn't depend on being in the same room. I could swear he almost added a 'so there' after that!

I have always 'travelled' at times, but it was only after reading about techniques for this used in Shamanism, I began to do so consciously. Geoff helped me in this and it made quite a difference in my remembering details of our work and adventures. If at times, some anxiety diminishes this ability, he boosts my memory by putting scenes in my mind. He calls this a sort of telepathic virtual reality. Often, once I have that 'start', the remainder floods back into my conscious mind.

In November 1996, Geoff was tremendously excited. He had found the home he wanted! He couldn't wait to show me and we travelled there in meditation. There was a house, centrally situated, and the rest mainly grass, beautiful vivid green. Over to one side was a large pond; a path meandering around this led into a woodland area. He said it had everything he wanted and as he described the beginnings of what he wanted to create there, I could visualise it taking shape and knew it would become a paradise of immense beauty, tranquillity and peace. In the months since, I have been privileged to watch it develop and grow, and see how immensely happy Geoff is, working on what he enjoys most of all.

# Chapter Three

# Geoff - My Own Experience

I have no exact memory of the moment I left the physical world. We all have our ways of going through the process and mine blotted out the actual transition. This often happens when it is quick as there isn't time for preparation and adjustment. One minute here, the next, where?

I woke, so it seemed, in a pleasant hospital, very confused and sleepy. I had no idea what had happened beyond feeling unwell, a period of what appeared like darkness but was somehow comfortable, and then being here. For a period of unknown time, I drifted in and out of consciousness. At different points, I was vaguely aware of someone sitting with me, and of others standing observing. Apart from this drowsiness, I felt very well.

Not everyone sleeps through the transition. Some simply move out of the physical body as easily as taking off a garment. Those sufficiently aware know right away what has happened, and are not surprised to find themselves just as complete as before, with a fully functioning etheric body the replica of the physical one they have just discarded. I have been told that where the passing is accompanied with great pain however, unless a painful experience is required, the entity is lifted out of the physical body before the actual 'death'. The physical body is capable of continuing for some time but will have no real consciousness. It is worth mentioning here, that animals also have this ability to remove themselves from painful endings and many who give service as 'prey' animals, do just that.

As the drowsiness began to lessen, I took more notice of my surroundings. The 'hospital' was airy, light and very peaceful. It was ground floor and through windows I could see a verandah outside and gardens beyond. It looked beautiful and worthy of closer inspection. Still confused, I puzzled over the lack of 'hospital smell', of frantic nurses and doctors rushing around with equipment, not being given any medicines, even of there being few other people there, and why I was still wearing the same clothes! Yet it all looked somewhat familiar; as did the crazy lady sitting with me, holding my hand and trying to convince me I had passed over! What nonsense, I thought, and attempted to assure her it wasn't so, couldn't possibly be, as she would see when my family visited me. I was also a bit worried because I couldn't remember the exact nature of my relationship with this lady - would I have any explaining to do!

Gradually things became clearer. I realised this couldn't be an earthly hospital, it was quite different. The sense of peace gives a timeless ambience which both refreshes and recharges. It has a healing quality of its own, and this is boosted by guides and other visitors, some of whom like ourselves, journey here during sleep to perform just this type of dedicated service, helping those who are 'displaced' come to terms with what has happened to them.

It is not easy to explain the absence of any time structure. On Earth, we are so controlled by time. Here, we have no such regime to adhere to, yet there is a kind of awareness of physical time for those remaining near Earth. I had no way of knowing how long I'd been 'recovering'. I have been told since, it took the equivalent of five days before I gained full perception of my new state of being, and recognised completely that this 'hospital' was the building I had visited many times during sleep, to help others in the same way I was now being helped, and that the lady who kept vigil beside me during that time, had been a co-worker with me during sleep for many years, sadly, completely without any waking consciousness of this for either of us. In fact, I would go as far as saying, had anyone told me of this other existence during my just ended lifetime, I would probably have considered them completely round the bend, and not hesitated to tell them so! However, I will attempt to explain this 'service', one of many that takes place nightly, often totally, obliviously, unknown to the dedicated workers, in more detail further on.

So here I was, all confusion now gone, and feeling fitter and much younger than for some time; in fact, disgustingly healthy. As I began to accept all this, we sat together outside and talked, on the verandah, also frequently strolled through the gardens, a pastel haven arranged with a perfection to delight all the senses, sheer joy to behold. Eventually awareness dawned enough for me to go on to the next stage, moving on from this haven to begin in earnest, life beyond the physical. There is never any pressure exerted to do so, but at a certain point of acceptance and adjustment, it is simply the obvious thing to do.

I was met by a guide, one of the evolved beings who works alongside us, and taken on to what are often described as the realms of light. Here, further recuperation takes place and adjustment for this other way of living. Perhaps readjustment is a better term since we have all been there before, many times, although usually at a lower level as each lifetime progresses us, if we have learned, as this is the purpose for physical life. There were many conversations with guides detailing various possibilities and other things during this time, but always these were helpful, friendly and humourous. These guides have known us throughout our lives and are there even if we are not actively working. Appointed to us before we are born, rarely are we aware of them in our conscious state, accepting their gentle guidance as intuition or whatever. I also met with relatives and friends who had 'died' before me, and they too helped me adjust, showed me around, and described their own lives in this dimension, helping me decide what I wanted to do now. It was a very pleasant time of reunions and decisions, of beginning to access other lives and review the one just finished. This is by no means any kind of 'judgement day' so advocated by some of the religious factions. We are never forced to do anything and all this reviewing is undertaken when we wish it. Most are eager to see how they have progressed although there are inevitably always regrets for intentions not realised, for things that were not fulfilled, even though we know there will always be other chances, other lives to complete all these things. For myself, there were among other things, regrets for a certain lack of awareness which may have resulted in me doing some things differently.

Throughout this period I lived in a room in what could loosely be described as a hostel. It is not essential to have a house to live in but on this level, most prefer to do so. I remained in this 'hostel' until I decided on, and found a home to suit me. The 'hostel' was not any kind of institution as the word may convey, but actually a large comfortable country house surrounded by its own gardens, and wonderful woods, countryside and scenery, providing plenty of scope for walking and exploring, which I did joyfully. We had our own rooms for privacy, a central room to congregate for discussions, meetings etc., and plenty of places outside to be alone with your thoughts. And believe me, there are a lot of those to contend with. I sat often in the gardens, thinking my thoughts; or with guides and friends, talking out things I needed to work through as part of the adjustment, as well as coming to terms with things I didn't fulfil.

During this period, I accessed all memories of the unconscious work undertaken during my last lifetime, and it was in the course of this, rediscovered the long-standing role of my co-worker who so ably helped me over the initial trauma of transition. I also learned, that she was still in the physical world, not on this side as I had believed, and in a degree of despair at the turmoil of her own life, that nobody was able to get through to her in any way. All they could do, interference not being an option unless in exceptional circumstances, was watch and wait, hoping something would lift her vibrations sufficiently to allow guidance again. Immediately I knew what it was I wanted to do, had to do, next. For various reasons, time in earthly terms was critical if she was to be brought back from the brink of an awful existence that could go on indefinitely. I already knew of the bond between us that went back thousands of years, and through many lifetimes, so who else could be better placed to help? I requested this option of the guide and although told it may well prove fruitless, it was a challenge, something I always enjoyed, and I was determined to give it my best shot.

Having decided on a course of action, my first task would be actually getting through to her. My first attempt was psychically and if it hadn't been for the importance of timing, it would have been comical! We do not automatically have supreme knowledge of everything once the physical is shed. Nor do we necessarily have instant memory from previous times. Instruction therefore comes from guides, but only by practise do we perfect methods of contact and communication. It isn't a whole lot different to physical life really, and wouldn't it be terribly boring to know everything just like that? Nothing new to learn or try for yourself! Paradise would get pretty tedious rather quickly like that!

It is quite frustrating trying to make yourself known to someone who is oblivious to your presence, and my first attempt was just like that. When their 'inner' sight and hearing are closed down to that extent, and you resort to frantic 'signals' hoping something will register, you can end up feeling just a trifle idiotic! Realising I was getting nowhere, I gave up and returned to my own dimension to rethink my plans. I thought it would be so easy after our time at the 'hospital' following my transition, or at least that it would be easier than it was, but undaunted, I was now even more determined to succeed.

In those early days, it was also exhausting for my new form to cope with the density of the physical world, and my energies needed restoring frequently. Thankfully this is something achieved quite simply here.

Although totally shut down in most other ways, the one spiritual element my friend still clung to was the rescue work. I knew this from consulting our helpful guide who informed me she would always accept 'jobs' when they arose, but refused to discuss anything else whatsoever. Something had removed all her trust and that saddened me very much. By this time, I remembered completely how well we always worked together, often anticipating each other so harmoniously that little additional instruction was needed.

A little inspiration took me to arrange with two other regular workers still in the physical world, an approach during sleep much in the way the work had been carried out. Success was by no means definite but we did it by slightly devious methods on the basis that the ends justify the means. A 'job' therefore was suggested and once accepted by her, the vibration of the other two ensured between us, we could persuade her to listen. Fortunately, this time everything went well, better than I'd hoped, and I knew I'd managed to lift her sufficiently out of the blackness for my second attempt to be easier. I did however, try another psychic effort in between, and failed miserably again!

Following two more successful contacts in that form, and gently persuading her to take up meditation regularly, it wasn't long before my own strength returned, my energies grew and developed, and we were able to communicate in other ways, including psychically. This was a beginning, and a marvellous one, leading to us working on this book to attempt to bring a greater understanding on all aspects of life in other dimensions.

Always remember, there is no reason why successful communication and co-operation between dimensions shouldn't take place. The problem is always from the physical side. The dense nature of the physical dimension makes it difficult for sustaining contact because of the 'invisible' aspect. In fact, we are not invisible to those who have developed the art of 'seeing', but humans in physical form are a trifle lazy. The lack of stimulus - seeing, hearing, etc., plus what seems 'real' around you, in the busy lives all lead today, means that which appears insubstantial is soon neglected and overlooked. It is something that needs working at and unfortunately, materialism takes precedence when the spiritual requires dedicated attention in times of quietness. Often this can be hard to attain in the noisy bustling physical world.

Many people I am sure, will say they have no awareness of those in spirit. Others may 'sense' something although sometimes this might just be an 'essence' of the departed person, left behind as a comforter. Most of us do 'look in' occasionally on former family and close friends. However, it is important to remember we do have our lives to get on with here. Much as some might like to believe, we don't sit around just watching forever more, and perhaps more important, those still on earth must let go and get on with their own lives. There is one inaccuracy that seems prevalent on earth, that those grieving can somehow 'hold on' to us and hamper our progress. In fact, it is the other way round. Once free of the physical nothing can hold us back or prevent us doing what we wish, going where we wish, or being with whoever we wish. However, there are some who try to 'hang on' to those still incarnate and this can explain some 'hauntings', but those entities soon learn the error of that. No, the main problem with those still on earth trying to hold on to what is past and done, is that they hold themselves back and block their own progress. Grieving is important of course, it is the natural way to heal and release yourself from that attachment. Excessive grief however can make those here feel a sense of discomfort, a pull, but it still doesn't hold us back. Once the grief is worked through, then the intention must be to get on with life, attracting new learning and experiences in keeping with your purpose in being on earth at any given time. Hard as it may be to accept, that experience of loss could be exactly the lesson you needed, chose and agreed to, for karmic or other reasons, and your personal responsibility is to ensure you don't allow it to block the good flow of life that awaits you following the successful conclusion of such lessons.

One of the first things to be learned at these levels, is that the majority of the major relationships during your life, are for karmic reasons and cannot continue in the same form here. That doesn't lessen them in any way, they are important, but there would be no movement beyond if everything stayed the same. I realise this will not seem acceptable to many who will argue about emotions involved.

All I can say is that without the emotions created, the relationships would not take place and the purposes would not be fulfilled. Your years in earthly incarnations may seem long, but in cosmic terms, they are only the blink of an eyelid, and as you soon realise on passing, your true life and home is in this form and these dimensions. If things stayed just the same as they were on earth, the Universe would soon grind to a halt because there would be no progress, no flow. This is nothing to be concerned about, any truly bonded links will continue, and anything else is adequately sorted out when you make your transition into these realms. A transition which is truly joyful and nothing to fear whatsoever.


## Rescue Work

This would seem to be the right place to describe this work and what it entails. First, whatever beliefs you may hold and harbour, there is nobody in physical life who does not 'travel' during their sleeping time. The vast majority have absolutely no waking recollection of this; some have dreams which seem not quite as normal, more 'real' than dreams usually are; some have flashes of memory, but without exception, all do so. Even ardent insomniacs, albeit more briefly, and without those regular, replenishing and purposeful visits to the spirit world, you could not continue to maintain your physical body which would seize up and die.

It is extremely rare for anyone to have complete recollection because the return to the physical body involves a certain loss due to density, affecting memory. It is however, our constant link to the world that is our real home and state of being. Our lifetimes, incarnations, are just the blink of an eyelid in cosmic terms. Periods of learning/experiencing to advance us evolutionally and to progress us spiritually. While our physical bodies sleep, our etheric selves return to these realms to be taught, to arrange things which then manifest in the physical world, and to discuss things with our guides and helpers. These are not journeys over some vast areas of space, but merely a slip into another dimension. There are various other things undertaken during this time, and one of these is to do work we are uniquely equipped for, having studied for this purpose, also during sleep.

We choose to do this work because there is a great need for it, but also because at certain levels, we can advance at a greater rate because we are helping others. A kind of spiritual brownie points system if you will. Usually the agreement to undertake rescue work is made here just before we are born, and there are many who do so.

Along with others forming part of our soul group, we trained for this work throughout 1978/9 during sleep, to then be unleashed into active service from 1980. The work we undertake falls into two types, 'mission' work, which entails going into hostile situations such as war zones, disaster zones etc., to help 'round up' newly departed souls for guides to take on into the light. These souls in such situations are so fearful and disorientated, often angry and filled with hate too, that they can end up on lower astral worlds ruled by negativity so bleak, it takes enormous periods of time for them to free themselves, and does damage which has a result in eventual subsequent incarnations. The physical world is in a bad enough state now with all the various damage inflicted on it, there are real risks if this work wasn't attempted. It requires those from both sides because sometimes these souls can only relate to the vibration of those still in the physical, still attached by the cord to their physical bodies.

The other type of work is in buildings such as the one we refer to as the Halfway House, where I was brought on passing. Here, those at an appropriate level dependent on how they lived their lives, find themselves; usually not realising they have passed over. It can take a very long time for some to awaken to the facts. One gentleman we helped took over two years in earth-time before realisation dawned and he could be taken on to recuperate and really begin his new life. Here we usually work in pairs, whereas the 'mission' work is always in groups.

Some of the work is extremely unpleasant in terms of witnessing the very worst of human degradation. This is another reason why those undertaking this work, rarely remember it on waking. It would be hard to bear, even risky to the physical mental state, without the awareness and understanding gained through the wider perception in these realms. This is something I have had to acknowledge since being here and working in full consciousness from this side.

When a 'job' arises, guides either 'collect' us, or we are informed subconsciously and gather at a predetermined location. Understand, whether a believer or not, we are always in touch with those assigned to guide and help us throughout our earthly lives; for the unaware at subconscious level. The cord attaching us to our physical body throughout life, filters all the information of what we experience, back, and this acts as a protection, keeping us from remembering the worst things. The only outward physical sign is perhaps an occasional unexplained restless night and slight weariness next day. All the information is stored in our subconscious minds for eventual assessment when we ourselves make our own transition into these realms.

It is vital for those involved in this work to be in complete harmony, in tune enough to anticipate with split second timing. Telepathy is common to this because often there isn't time to discuss how to proceed. Things happen at a much faster rate in other vibrations, and hesitations can mean losses of those we are there to help. Therefore we work with those on the same level, and from the same groups who are closely linked, having the same aims and ideals. I will attempt to explain about soul groups in another chapter.

Don't think this work occurs every night during sleep. Although our etheric selves need no sleep as such, we do require rest even when free from the physical state. In the same way, when first arriving over here, we have to build up to comfortable energy levels, even more so if there has been a long difficult illness. And from time to time, we still need rest to restore those levels. Those doing this work while in the physical, may for example, be called once or twice a week for a few months, then not again for several more months. It all depends on what arises and since life on Earth is not pre-destined, our particular skills could be required at any time. In between those times, we rest or are free to do other things while our physical bodies sleep, including 'travelling' for pleasure. No doubt you find that hard to accept because unless you are 'awakened' and fully aware, you simply don't remember. But we are all far more than just physical beings, which is all science can measure at the moment, and the sleep/dreaming state is still shrouded in mystery along with the majority of our brain's ability. There will no doubt be those 'specialists' who will claim they know it all, but this is only a form of mass control, something I will write about separately. Accepting the possibility that while your physical body sleeps, your true self experiences in other dimensions, will open your mind to begin remembering. In a sense, it could be said each and every one of us leads a 'double' life, but only the truly fortunate and open minded ones, recall any part of their spiritual side while still incarnate.

There are various other types of rescue work, handled by those suitably trained. There are always thousands of lost wandering souls clinging to Earth, unable to find their way home because they have no belief in any afterlife, and they all need rescuing. It can be a very distressing sight to see the fears holding these people back and make no mistake, by no means do we all get there automatically. Those 'lost' in this way can wander for ages trying to make contact with relatives, friends, acquaintances even, not understanding what has happened to them and why nobody sees or hears them. They cannot believe they have 'died' because they were so certain death ended everything. Think about spending a day with everyone ignoring you and not showing any sign of you being there, this is the normal experience for those convincing themselves nothing exists after death, and it continues until that belief is altered sufficiently for some light to shine through. What damage these 'experts' do then, in denying the possibility even, of continuance! A slight consolation is that they too will have that same post death experience, and what a shock it will be to them. However, for all, help is always available no matter what misguided beliefs lead to such awful confusion. Imagine the relief!

Other types of this work include the very hazardous entry into the lowest realms, to bring out trapped souls and lead them to the light. This is not undertaken lightly and only advisable with the strongest of guides. This form of rescue work is usually for those higher up in the evolutionary stakes, certainly above the levels we have attained, and often, they reincarnate just for that purpose, again because a physical source is required to reach those souls.

It may seem rather strange all this goes on around you, unseen, and that you could even be part of it without consciously knowing. Be wary therefore of arrogantly dismissing anything you cannot truly understand. We probably all do so from time to time, but with a slightly more open mind you will, like myself, also discover one day, the wonderful possibilities which are limitless. What fools we can be in the physical world, to shut ourselves off from our marvellous 'other world' experiences by allowing a restricting of our minds.

# Chapter Four

# A Wealth of Confirmation

Throughout the time Geoff has been in contact with me, and particularly at the beginning, I asked constantly for proofs and confirmations. I wanted to be absolutely certain all I was experiencing was genuine, and that he was who he said he was. He never once objected and provided me with so many confirmations, it wasn't long before I had no doubts whatsoever and lost all my scepticism.

Many of the proofs he gave were small things which only had meaning to me, but there were also some larger things, some quite spectacular and tangible. It is these I will describe, and hopefully convey the sense of wonder I felt, and gratitude that he went to such lengths to impress on me the reality of all this. It seemed that every few months, just when I was wavering slightly, he would create or attract something major to pull me back on line, fast.

However, I did learn early on, it was a great mistake to challenge him too far! One day, feeling rather negative and disbelieving, I dared him to convince me he was there! A little later, I wrote up my daily diary entry recording experiences and things we had talked about. Suddenly, the machine switched on to reformatting the disk, wiping the disk and with it, six months of entries! This operation is impossible to do by accident as there are a couple of stages to go through before the actual reformatting begins. I tried every which way to repeat what had happened, and couldn't do so. I was furious! I told him exactly what I thought about him doing that. When I calmed down, I realised it wasn't actually as bad as I first thought. Much of what was on the disk, I had in note form. Most of the detailed information he had given was on a separate disk, and all that was really lost, were some personal things he had told me of his life here which maybe, were better not recorded anyway. When I came to re-do the disk again, I found many things very easily remembered in complete detail, which, since I do not have a photographic memory, I could only think he had relented and helped me recall through telepathy. It was an enormous task of collating and retyping though which occupied many hours. I vowed never to risk such a challenge again, and also to keep a back up disk. A couple of times since, when I have been perhaps a bit too cheeky, I ask him please not to mess up the word processor again, just in case!

One other time that was slightly traumatic, happened before that, late in 1996. On that occasion I was doubting his ability to be able to do anything should I be in actual danger of any kind. The following day I was at the top of the stairs and as I started down, both my feet slipped off the stairs, although the sandals I wore had excellent non-slip soles! For a fraction of a second I was actually suspended in the air, then I was caught, my feet replaced firmly on the stair and my hand on the bannister. I don't doubt any more!

Those occasions aside, all the other confirmations were lovely, uplifting and joyful. The very first of these came in October, exactly six weeks after our first contact, and inspired the title of this book.

It was a lovely autumn day, gorgeous blue sky with only a few clouds drifting across it. A day that lifts the spirits anyway, but I didn't expect the miraculous sight I witnessed as I waited for a bus into town. The bus was due in about ten minutes and glancing up at the sky, I saw, spanning the width of the road, a large squarish cloud and tailing off bottom left of this, was a smaller oval cloud. As I focussed on this smaller cloud I became aware it was completely rainbow coloured! The whole cloud was all the colours present in a rainbow and it was edged in gold. It was breathtakingly beautiful and I have never seen anything remotely like it before. The larger cloud it emerged from had no hint of any of this colour whatsoever. I stared at it for ages, then wondered if any of the others queuing at the stop had noticed it. There were seven other people besides myself. Although most were facing this phenomenon, they appeared oblivious to it. Surely I couldn't be the only one who could see it? The cloud was still there and just as brightly coloured. It didn't fade throughout the time I waited for the bus. Seeing it gave me such a feeling of pure joy, a cosmic sensation which remained, and I floated through the rest of the day, my heart singing. I have always loved rainbows, their magical quality seems to hold promises of mysterious things from other worlds. I'd been seeking a physical manifestation to confirm my contact. This cloud gave me that and seemed to promise much more awaited me.

That experience was a turning point for me. It swept away finally, the remaining blackness and niggles of doubt that plagued me. I accepted all that was happening was wonderful and Divinely orchestrated for some yet to be revealed purpose.

I will never forget the sight of that cloud, more beautiful than anything I have ever seen before. It was the first impressive confirmation jolting me out of the mundane. Although I did go through subsequent periods of querying and occasional resistance, boosted from time to time by minor proofs, I still remembered that with a sense of wonder. Then in January, I received another strange happening to further confirm my experiences.

Friends in Glastonbury produce a magazine called *UFO Reality* which covers all aspects of unexplained alien phenomena. Having been supportive of our animal charity since 1991, they kindly sponsor an advertisement for us in this magazine, inviting donations. In January 1997, I received a letter from North of the Polar Circle, from someone who had received a copy of the magazine containing our advertisement. The content however, brought complete amazement.

The writer explained he channelled an ascended master and had done so for six years. This ascended master wished a message to be given to me - 'they are sorry things are made invisible by the 'illuminati!' A strange message indeed and one having nothing to do with our brief advertisement. However, just prior to that message arriving, I had been complaining and questioning just why the spirit realms are so hidden from us and all to do with those worlds, cannot be more visible! Even stranger, I wrote back to my correspondent, thanking him for taking the time to write with this message. A couple of weeks later, my letter was returned, unable to be delivered as the address couldn't be found!

Startling experiences like this, happening when they do and having relevance, serve to remind us there is far more out there than can be explained away rationally. And I consider attempting to do so is an insult. Opening our minds brings rewards more valuable than anything this material dimension can offer. Some seem unable to accept anything unless it is adequately proven. To who's satisfaction? Not those experiencing since there is nothing as adequate as personal experience.

During summer 1997 Geoff learned and perfected another method of contact and one which is undeniably tangible. I discovered quite early on he is very resourceful and deter-mined to communicate in every way he can. It took me a while to realise what he was doing - he never tells me if something new is coming up in case I anticipate. To do so could block his attempts.

It didn't dawn on me at first, that the extraordinary amount of light flickers and flashes had anything to do with Geoff. I already knew he was capable of manipulating electricity which, I suppose, being another 'invisible' energy form, makes it ideal for spiritual purposes. When it did occur to me that there seemed to be an intelligence involved in the light signals - they followed me from room to room - I queried if it was him, and immediately had an answering flash. I said hello, and there was another, (probably along with a sigh of relief that I had finally realised!).

Since that dawning it has gone from strength to strength. Every evening now he signals in varying amounts, as many as twenty-three when I have been feeling low, just four or five at other times. Only once since he began them, was there an evening without any, and this, he informed me later, was because he needed the energy for something else he was perfecting.

The element of practise required in most forms of contact is obvious, as well as the ability to tune in to wherever I am. I have tested this. Although the timings of the signals vary completely every evening, now and then one certain time seems to be favoured. As time, in our terms, doesn't exist in other dimensions, I presume it fits in with whatever Geoff is doing. Where maybe one particular time has produced a signal for two or three evenings, I make a point of walking into another room just before that time, and sure enough, the light in that room has flashed at the exact time.

Practise means Geoff can now control the signals so well they are given very deliberately, as recently when there were five carefully controlled flashes one after the other in the space of a minute. He did however admit to me that at first, he had to be very careful not to overdo the energy used and fuse the lot! These signals mean a lot to me. It is tangible evidence, something outside of myself completely, and something he can do wherever I am - they have occurred in shops and other places too - and to me, represents a constant link not unlike a regular telephone call, something that seems to say; 'I am here, and thinking of you.'

Right from the start, Geoff told me he is only a whisper away and if I need him urgently, I must call and he would be with me immediately. Once or twice I have had to test him on that and he has never let me down. I worry about disturbing him, and whatever he is working on at the time, but he never appears to mind.

Not long after those first contacts, when the meditations were going well, we had discussed suicide. I asked him what he would do if I decided I wanted out? He said he would attempt to prevent it although none can if we are determined enough. A day or so later, walking back from posting a letter, I saw a coach approaching fast, and thought, it would be quite easy just to step out, it would have no chance of missing me on the narrow country roads. It was only an idle thought without intention, but at that moment, I distinctly felt hands on my shoulders, holding me back. I couldn't step forward at all! Now I'm for it, I thought, this will be another lecture! But no, he was very concerned and thought he had let me down in some way, for me to be thinking like that. I felt dreadful and vowed never to think that way again, even idly.

Twice in the autumn, about two months apart, Geoff succeeded in fully materialising. This was not solidly, but a little like a hologram in that he was almost transparent, but very much consciously there. The whole effect was surrounded in a white mist or light which has something to do with an output of the energies required. These each lasted long enough for me to take in every detail before gradually fading.

Geoff has attempted to explain to me how those in spirit forms can use atoms and molecules here, 'borrowing' them to create images of themselves which we can see physically. Not being technically minded I haven't fully understood this. I have a better idea though, after another type of materialisation he perfected. All that we think of as solid around us is not in fact so. Everything, tables, chairs, walls etc., are made up of atoms and molecules, held together by thought and other things, once created. An automatic process which we take for granted and don't even fully understand. On one occasion my attention was drawn to a section of wall, quite plain and painted a very pale blue. As I watched this, part of the wall seemed to fragment. It shimmered into a mass of small black particles. The second time it did this, the particles formed themselves into a pale shadow, the size and shape of a human head. Unlike normal shadows where no details can be made out within it, I could see features in this, hair, eyes, nose, and mouth, which was smiling. It was also animated just like normal faces. Starting off almost in profile it turned until facing me squarely on. I clearly recognised Geoff without doubt. This materialisation lasted about two minutes before fading back to normal wall.

Throughout my life I have had occasional startling things happen, although nothing like the concentration of events as in that first year of contact. Something happened in August 1997 which to this day, still fills me with amazement, and proves nothing really is impossible now. It cannot be chance either that it was August, a month that had such meaning to Geoff in earthly terms.

At the end of September 1996, our charity found a promoter who organised a competition selling tickets to raise funds for us. He advertised for agents to sell the tickets all over the country. The promotion actually ended the following July but advertisements obviously remained in various places.

In August 1997, we received a telephone call from a lady who had seen the advertisement in her local veterinary clinic. Being interested in helping animals, she took down the details. However, when she tried the number, which was in Yorkshire, she got nothing. Thinking she had written down the digits incorrectly, she decided to try other combinations of the number. Eventually she got a connection, someone in London! It is at this point the whole thing moves into the mystical. The person she contacted in London was a friend of mine. Someone who originally contacted me in 1992 seeking healing for her dog, having previously seen and kept an article in The Guardian about me giving healing to animals! We have corresponded since then.

I am certain statisticians would put enormous odds against such a chance occurrence but would regard it as totally impossible when considering the two numbers differed completely by two digits! But to me, it confirmed wonderfully the reality of all I was experiencing and nothing could be ruled out as impossible now.

Once my meditations with Geoff were well established and regular, I soon discovered we could link up and talk at any time without needing the relaxation, concentration and altered state of meditation. This started early in November 1996. Having completed a meditation and immersed in a very interesting discussion, my consciousness fully back in the physical, he told me to open my eyes and just continue talking. This I did and we talked on quite naturally for some time. It was only later I realised I had been perfectly aware of him and seen him, although at that stage, only through my third eye located at the brow chakra.

Since then we have developed this aspect too. We still do daily meditations as these allow for wider scope within that discipline, but also, we daily link up at other times just to walk and talk together, and to work on this book.

I find it quite impressive just what is possible in contact with those in other dimensions. We have been so conditioned through the ages, programmed with limitations and restrictions, frightened with dire warnings and generally misled. I wouldn't condone anyone 'dabbling' with such things out of idle curiosity, but where there is an inner feeling and interest, I would urge seeking and development. There are many on this path who can guide and help, as well as the spirit guides we all have while incarnate. Always seek the light and genuine highest ideals, and there is no danger.

Very early in January 1997 I had the flu prevalent at that time. For several days I did little but sleep and rest, and my greatest comfort was in finding Geoff there frequently, seemingly watching over me. On one occasion when I'd slept for rather a long time, I was awakened by the back of fingers gently stroking my cheek. I could even hear the gentle brush of this in front of my ear. The minute I woke fully it stopped suddenly and I asked why? He told me they are not allowed to do anything which might frighten us. I emphasised nothing like that would frighten me and I found it further evidence of his presence.

One aspect perplexed me, so many speak of contacts with those from spirit being accompanied by chills and cold. I have never found this to be so with Geoff, quite the opposite in fact. I have little tolerance to cold, and get really miserable if feeling cold. My home is not well heated and many a winter, have had to resort to cuddling a hot water bottle to stop me shivering. Not so any more however. Whenever Geoff is around there is warmth, sometimes a glow of warmth I can actually reach out and locate. And I have come across this phenomenon since, in correspondence from others experiencing at a similar level.

I have gained so much from this contact; knowledge, a tremendous expansion of awareness, improvements in all areas of my psychic abilities, and wonderful memories of astral travelling between dimensions and to places and experiences I thought would not be achieved in this lifetime. Plus the bonus of fascinating, funny, wonderful, shared companionship which is so strong, I often and easily forget Geoff is not actually here physically now. To me he is, and remains always, very much still alive.

# Chapter Five

# Geoff - Relationships and Soul Groups

I realise this will be a difficult subject for some to accept, and one that may be uncomfortable. However, when there are so many living in spent, unsatisfactory relationships, it can give hope to know the reasons, and that nothing is ever lost forever, or goes on forever. Even when a relationship is good and reasonably compatible, would you necessarily want to think of it lasting beyond life, and maybe for eternity?

It is not my intention for you to feel you have to accept anything that may cause pain. Your relationships, whatever category they fall into, are important. It is through them, you learn, experience, and grow. Grow in the spiritual sense; that which is required for progress. Your closest relationships will be drawn from the pool of the soul group. All within that group feel attraction and affection for every other member of that group. This is one of the few things decided on before incarnating. The purpose for your life is decided, by you, and those who can help achieve that purpose, as well as achieve whatever they require, agree to play a role in that life, with you. And that is what it is really, role playing. You take it on just as an actor takes a part. Shakespeare had it about right.

In the larger sense, the roles taken matter little because it is the purpose you set out to achieve which is the main criteria. In physical terms, that will no doubt sound selfish because you think only from the aspect of one lifetime. When you view several, and see those same players taking other roles, it gives a whole different outlook. Your review of your life thus, becomes an assessment of how you achieved your purpose, not how good, bad or indifferent your relationships were. That is of course, unless the interaction between you and another person was the resolving of karmic debts. These debts, cause and effect from other lifetimes, form the main reason for your closest relationships.

One example to illustrate; in a previous life you may have suffered because of a selfish, indifferent parent. Your lesson may have been to become your own person regardless. In the subsequent lifetime, you become the parent with a selfish, indifferent child, giving both the opportunity to learn through reversal of the roles. This is a very simplistic example, often the lessons are far deeper and more complex, and particularly where karma is involved. There may even be more than one thing to be achieved during your lifetime and it is a rare life that achieves them all. It is of no consequence because there are always other opportunities.

Lives are not pre-determined. There is no map taking you from the cradle to the grave with every major event sign-posted in red ink. If it were so we would not have free will and be nothing other than puppets dancing to some celestial tune. If that were so, physical beings wouldn't need minds and brains to think with because thoughts would be irrelevant, so would emotions. And it isn't like that at all. We decide before being born what lessons, experiences, karmic resolutions, we want to attempt. We then 'select' parentage and family conditions that give us a start in that, parentage and family which will mostly, be from our soul group and have taken the required roles to also achieve from that. As we move through life we attract and create according to our required lessons etc. But free will is paramount and often along the way, we alter things. Some lessons are hard, tough, and in human form, it is sometimes easier to avoid them. Human nature being what it is, we would continuously opt out if we knew all that life had in store in terms of experiences.

Physical life is made out to be the be all and end all. This is because of not remembering in between lives, and other lives. The frailty of physical form ensures this or we would all be totally confused. As it is, most of us have minds that most of the time, are a jumble of bits and pieces which rattle around, each having a turn in the front seat when necessary.

When some speak of physical life being like the school room, they are making a pretty good guess at the truth. It is like that, and while in physical form we are all pupils learning our trade, aiming for the top of the 'class'. Interactions thus with others, relationships, are our class project assignments. Some we complete satisfactorily, some we fail at, and some we miss out on altogether. Our 'end of term grades', our achievements; progress us, or if we don't fulfil some lesson, and it happens although rarely, we stay in the same 'class' until we pass our tests. Just as long as we do our best always, we cannot go far wrong.

The biggest conflict will arise, I am sure, in the area of marriage and similar close partnerships. Major importance is placed on these in earthly terms, but in fact, only very, very few are considered to be 'made in heaven', good reason to have a get out clause in the marriage ceremony - 'till death us do part!' The vast majority of these unions are purely for karmic balancing purposes and lessons. That is not to say you don't feel love for those who share your life so intimately. You would need to, or there would be no partnership and the purpose wouldn't be achieved. This is where life is really an illusion. How many marriages begin on high hopes, with a feeling of love you think will last forever, only to end a few years down the line, sometimes in extreme acrimony? But there is no failure because that was probably the way it was intended all along, the lesson learned, the balancing completed. A mutual resolution. The important part is to let go, and move on. That is essential. The reason for that experience having passed, you owe it to yourself to free yourself from it, and get on with your life as intended. There may be another waiting for what was agreed for the next stage in your life. But with free will, nothing can be forced. However, failure to fulfil your purpose may not only let yourself down, but that other also, and that is how some karmic debts occur because those agreed purposes must be achieved, if not in this lifetime, then in another.

Great changes are happening on earth at the moment and this requires the clearing of all the karmic emotional baggage accumulated through many incarnations. This is why so many are changing partners often and regularly, allowing for the 'debts' to be cleared. The new age will bring an important difference in relationships. Once free of the karmic cycles, we will all seek a lifelong partner with whom we can find total, lasting harmony and love. There will only be one and this is vital as we will be working for the planet and the good of all so the game-playing of karmic balancing and lessons cannot continue. The population must be controlled and there will be fewer children. These will be conceived, born and raised in such a completeness of love, they will be better balanced and whole themselves, ready to experience life properly in the correct vibration.

The above will be the way relationships evolve in physical terms, but what about in the other dimensions? Do you imagine relationships cease to be once the physical world is left behind?

We were never intended to make our journey through eternity alone. We even theorise here as to whether the Creator actually has or had a partner, an equal flame to share all of creation with at the beginning of it all, perhaps eventually merging into one complete union. Until we reach the higher levels, far off from where we are now, we won't know, but it seems likely. Why else would there be such an understanding of our need for companionship? Why create a perfect balance of male and female counterparts? Why else are we constantly told love is the most important quality of all, and the only thing we take with us from life to life?

We are all part of soul groups. When setting out, we do so with a purpose, a mission, and that alters according to many things. By the time we achieve human form in our incarnational rounds, we have separated into individual souls, to experience and learn. As I understand it, this separation takes place in stages, first half breaking away, then a quarter, and so on. But each separation makes ultimate divisions into pairs, and these pairs remain closely bonded for eternity, even though it may be a very long time before they share lifetimes together, or recognise each other, here, or on Earth. Those pairs are truly soul-mates in every sense, truly two halves of a complete union.

Other members of our soul group also have a strong bond, particularly those breaking away last, and these usually take roles in our lives to aid in learning etc. Thus, your mother, father, husband, wife, brother, sister, son, daughter, who form your family in this lifetime, will probably take another of those roles in some other lifetime and may well have done so in previous lives. When returning here, you will meet up again and reunions are joyful, but nothing is as strong or marvellous as finding your true soul-mate. And true soul-mates will be, and remain, lovers through many of the etheric levels here.

No doubt that will shock those of you who believe anything of that nature disappears once we pass over. Those who give information along those lines are not totally wrong either. It is just that they don't have the full picture. Information may be given by those on this side who have not yet met up with their true soul-mate and gained full understanding of that connection, or have not yet freed themselves from the limiting and restrictive beliefs created by those on Earth who seek to control. As they believe, so they will find, and as they find, so they will communicate those findings because that will be their experience here. Make no mistake, there is no lust or promiscuity, these true 'sins of the flesh' have no place on these levels, they are the lower negative sides of intimacy on earth. And most of our experiences of physical intimacy remain attached to the physical body, never touching the heart and soul, and left behind when we pass into these dimensions.

But the love and loving between true soul-mates is more profound and beautiful than anything experienced on earth, a complete shared union of body, heart and soul, a oneness that actually creates a link right back to The Source; and that bond is eternal. That expression of love is a 'gift' given by the Creator, can you really believe that same Creator would snatch it away again in these dimensions thus also violating our free will in the process?

There does seem to be some confusion about the term 'soul-mates'. Some sources say we have several but only one 'soul twin'. Others say there can only be one true soul-mate. Perhaps it would help to clarify if we look at the definition of the word 'mate'. It is defined as being a comrade/friend, or an intimate partner. So both theories are correct. While incarnate, we have several soul-mates (comrades/friends) who take on relationship roles for mutual learning and karmic balancing. This will include those who also form our intimate partnerships. But there is only one eternal soul-mate (intimate partner) who journeys with us in that relationship between lives, whether or not they took that rare role while incarnate.

When you can understand the role playing that is part of physical life, and the reasons for that, there is another aspect to consider - judgement. One thing humans are very good at doing, is judging their fellow beings, often harshly. But each of us knows why we are on Earth subconsciously, and the people we encounter along our way, whatever relationships we form, are all for a reason. It does no good therefore, to judge others whatever they do. Disapproval should be limited to not doing the same because it isn't your required experience or lesson; but to actively speak out or attempt to disrupt other's lives, is wrong. Never assume responsibility for others, being responsible for yourself is your only goal. Taking on responsibility for others' through interference, means taking on part of their karma too!

Soul groups evolve together although there may always be some ahead, and some behind, depending on how long it takes to learn certain lessons. This means sometimes, some of the group may move up several levels, and others may work with other groups with a similar purpose. However, this is rare with the smaller units the groups break down into. Their closeness means they tend to follow the same pathway, and their progress also follows mirroring patterns. When you meet someone in the physical dimension, and feel you have known them forever, finding much in common among interests and lifestyle, you can be pretty sure you have encountered one of your soul group members. Life-long friendships and relationships fall into this category too, no matter what crises may have to be faced. The traumas are incidental, part of the experiencing and learning we all take on to make those evolutionary steps. Nothing can stand still. If it did so, the entire Universe would grind to a halt. We are often told, it doesn't matter what happens to you in life, what matters is your reactions to those happenings. Those reactions either promote you, or hold you back. It is important to forget the word 'victim'. There is no such thing in spiritual terms. Every single event is arranged and agreed upon as you move through your life, prior to its manifestation. Nothing occurs by 'accident', but through subconscious choice for the entire purpose.

Let me take this a stage further. Accept that your physical body is just temporary, few can doubt that because it is well documented that after death, it gradually breaks down to component parts, some of which return to the elements of the earth. Think of it as the costume you wear for the role you are playing. And all that happens to you while incarnated, happens to your physical body. This applies whether the events are pleasant or awful. Nothing touches your spirit apart from the memories, stored similarly to a library, to refer to whenever the need arises. Your purpose on earth is to experience and bring back those events, assessing here, how well you reacted, how well you dealt with your life, how you interacted with those in that life, and, how you treated others. When you understand this fully, you no longer see yourself as a 'victim', but take full responsibility for yourself and your life. Then, and only then, can you create a life of your choosing, and not one foisted upon you by the controlling whims of others. Until now, most of us have been caught up in the karmic cycles, putting right the effects of allowing ourselves to be 'victim' or 'aggressor'. Lifetime after lifetime, round and round, crawling ahead pitifully slowly in any progressional terms, while we sort out all our karmic errors. That has to end now. The planet is in need of a total cleansing following centuries of abuse. We all have to raise our consciousness to take a step forward in evolution, finding a new way of living, relating, being. If we don't do so now, there may not be a future for Earth and her inhabitants. We have been systematically destroying the planet which nourishes and houses us, and the many warnings given on this, have been consistently ignored.

Mankind has been mostly lethargic in awakening to his responsibilities. In spiritual terms, it doesn't mean humans will cease to be, but without planet Earth, future lives would have to be taken on other worlds, in other places, and possibly, even in other forms. For many, this would be a hard adjustment to make. For some soul groups nearing the end of the incarnational round, it could be a set back in evolution. We all owe it to ourselves and the planet, to start getting it right, now, and that means beginning to look into life and death, and all that encompasses, in a new light of understanding. Old patterns of denial cannot be sustained any longer. A whole, new, delightful way of living and relating awaits us all, both in the physical dimension, and in the spiritual realms.

# Chapter Six

# Travelling and Treats - and Gifts!

Throughout my life I have often travelled spontaneously. Most people have heard the terms 'out of the body' experiences, and astral travel. This is what travelling is about, leaving the physical body during sleep or meditation, to visit other places including the realms of spirit. It is quite different from dreaming, however lucid those dreams are. The feeling in them is different, and dreams are usually three dimensional, whereas travelling is fourth dimensional.

Shamanism has techniques for conscious travelling and studying this helped me enormously, not only in controlling my travels, but also in remembering them on return. While we are still incarnate, a silver cord attaches us to our physical body although there is no awareness of this during our travels. This cord ensures our return into the physical. When we 'die', this cord severs and is absorbed, and our physical life is ended. Our awareness and consciousness is then totally in the spiritual dimension, part of our etheric form.

Everyone travels during sleep. Most have no memory of this at all on waking. My previous memories of travelling were limited to an odd memory and those completed during meditations. However, having learned of years of working with Geoff, and others, during sleep state, and been completely oblivious to this 'other life' we'd shared, I was determined to rectify this lapse in future. Gradually I am training myself to consciously recall everything. Sometimes 'life' gets in the way by causing anxieties which always diminish psychic abilities, but Geoff usually helps by putting a telepathic image in my mind to trigger memory. The only exception is when we have a rescue mission that is traumatic. These he insists, must remain subconscious because of the effect they may produce. No amount of persuasion will sway him on that.

Not long after the preliminaries of contact were established, Geoff asked me if I had any remaining ambitions or things I would like to do before leaving the physical world? There were two things dear to me, which I held as ambitions of sorts, one was to swim with dolphins, the other, to hold and hopefully cuddle, a koala bear.

The first of these Geoff arranged as a treat for me, on the night of December 26th 1996. It took place just off the Irish coast. The water was inky dark, lit only by moon and stars. Although it must have been cold, I felt only the wetness of it. There was one dolphin, and it was a most amazing experience. The memory of the smoothness of his skin was still with me when I woke in the morning. The friendly way he played and swam around me, nudged me, and communicated, I will never forget. There is a specialness about dolphins which leaves a feeling of unity and humility, which remains with you ever after.

The second of those ambitions was a treat for me on the night of Easter Monday 1997. This took place in a sanctuary for native animals, which Geoff said was in Queensland territory. Again, the memory was vivid. There were young kangaroos there too, and these could obviously see us. Animals have no logical minds to block natural abilities and therefore are far more aware of the other dimensions around them, and see spirit forms readily. The koala was a tame one. I held him while he munched on a piece of eucalyptus, and marvelled at the denseness of his fur and his soft eyes. Although a fairly brief visit, the memory of it remains clear months later.

Those who have no conscious memory of such experiences may find it difficult to imagine how they can be achieved. In the lighter dimensions, it is necessary only to think of a place you wish to be, mentally project yourselves to that place, and you are there in an instant. It is only in the heavy vibration of physical life and the density of our physical bodies lacking such freedom of movement, that we need vehicles to carry us from A to B. When our etheric bodies leave the physical during sleep, meditation, etc., we can then move with that same ease. Those who have no memory of doing so may dismiss it as imagination but that alone cannot give the clarity and sensation of such travels, particularly if it is something unknown to you before.

On the night of my birthday, February 6th 1997, Geoff arranged a party for me which was held in the gardens of the Halfway House. There were many guests, some I knew, some I had known but didn't recognise while still attached to the physical this time around. I'd spoken to him previously, of a former neighbour I'd been fond of, who had died three years before. As a surprise, Geoff had located him and he was also at the party, his lovely sense of humour still the same. We had a pleasant time catching up and reminiscing, and it was wonderful to see him again.

The interesting part about this particular treat was a confirmation I received a day or so afterwards. I knew about the party in advance and had asked if a particular friend, one who has someone close in spirit, could be taken to it by her companion. I made no mention of it to her and unfortunately, her own psychic abilities were very blocked by circumstances at the time. However, a day or so later, speaking to her, she said what a peculiar night she had that night resulting in her oversleeping and feeling tired and heavy next day. I then told her about the party she had attended. She commented that she obviously enjoyed herself and what a shame she couldn't consciously remember it!

I had another very interesting confirmation following another travelling experience. It is startling ones like this, that I find completely convincing.

In 1994 I went into hospital for a triple hernia repair operation. During the time I was unconscious, some four hours, I recall only a blackness, a void. It was as if I'd totally lost four hours somehow. I didn't like it and as I was on a downward spiral at the time, wondered if that was what death was like! Logic told me as I was aware of that blackness, it could hardly be so, but fear took over from reason and I began to believe that could have been what I was experiencing then.

At the end of January 1997, I went in as a day patient for a very simple, routine operation on my leg. Recalling my earlier experience I was determined for it not to happen again, and I asked Geoff if he could make sure I left my physical body and went off to enjoy myself while the operation took place. The day patients were divided into those before lunch and those after, I was an after, checking into the day ward at 2 p.m. The doctor came round to check health was sound enough for the operation to proceed, then came a fairly long wait for to go down to theatre. During this wait, I became aware of Geoff's presence and from that moment, I was completely calm and relaxed. I even joked with the anaesthetist's assistant as she wheeled the trolley down.

Fortunately the operation was so minor no pre-med was given. Equally so, the anaesthetist explained exactly what he was doing in advance which gave time for me to be ready. Geoff had prepared me to leave my body just before the anaesthetic took effect. As the anaesthetic was injected in and Geoff said now, I felt myself getting longer, or so it seemed, until I thought I would drop off the end of the trolley! I realised I was leaving through my head, something I don't usually do. In seconds, I was standing beside Geoff, next to the trolley, looking down at myself; now sleeping. What a strange feeling it gives to see yourself like that. It brings it home how much more there is to all beings than just the one form.

We wasted no time in getting away from there - I had no wish to see myself being operated on! Geoff had not said where he would take me as we were not certain I would succeed in my attempt. I closed my eyes for the actual journey and when I opened them, we stood in front of Geoff's home. Although when he first found it, he took me in meditation to see the pond and area where he aimed to create gardens, I hadn't seen the house. It was more beautiful than I'd pictured from his description. The natural stone of the walls seemed almost alive, breathing. It is not a huge house but is roomy and spacious. The front door opens onto a large square hall, on each side of this, three rooms lead off, one large, two small. The large room on the right, is a living room, cosily carpeted and completed with two large and comfortable, cream settees. Stairs go up middle back of the hall and around the upper floor is a gallery overlooking the hall below. Rooms lead similarly off from this and are exactly as you would find in a physical dimension house. The back wall upstairs has a large window which looks out over the rear gardens. Downstairs, there is a conservatory along the back wall, now clothed in an amazing selection of plants rich in colour and scent.

Following a quick look around the house, Geoff told me to wait in the hall and he had someone for me to meet. He returned with two dogs, one which had been his own and whom he described as 'a wonderful friend with whom he could share secrets he could never tell another human'; the other was Shane, my German Shepherd I lost in 1994 at just six years old! He had been allergic to wheat, developed epilepsy at three, and following an operation to remove bladder stones, liver cancer had been found and he wasn't resuscitated. I cannot describe what an emotional moment that was, for all of us. For some time after Shane died, he had come back, I was aware of him, always accompanied by a unique 'doggy' aroma. But he hadn't visited for some time and to see him, fuss him again, was bliss.

We all went for a walk along a path to the right of the house, past fields and round to the wildlife pond, and along the path through the woods beyond. Such tranquillity filled the air, and a beauty almost impossible to describe in earthly vocabulary. Everywhere the colours were so vibrant and the light, like a golden, perfect summer day. It was even more than that, a feeling of total freedom, security, not overshadowed by the need to pay for anything - there is no money, all is done by co-operation and mutual exchange. The negative things that make life here so stressful, just don't have a place there.

Returning from our walk to the house, Geoff then said it was time for me to go back. I knew by now that I wanted to stay, so much. It was where I wanted to be, where I belonged. But he said I must go back, it wasn't quite time for me yet. I tried so hard to persuade him to let me stay, not to make me go back, but I knew really it was unfair, it couldn't be his decision and I had to give in. I made a final fuss of Shane and the next thing I knew, I woke up back in the ward.

As my eyes took in the dreary walls, the ceiling, the other beds, I was aware I could still feel Shane's fur on my hand, and such an overwhelming sense of sadness filled me with the desire to cry and cry. I didn't want to be here anymore. I wanted so much to go back to that place that was home, and where I felt happier than I have ever felt here.

**72**

I hadn't been conscious long when the anaesthetist came to see me, something unusual after an operation. He looked a worried man. He wanted to check I was all right. Apparently I should only have been under for about half an hour, but they couldn't rouse me. I had been out for two and a half hours! All the other day patients had gone home, I was the last one there. The unit should have closed at six but it was nearly seven thirty before I finally left. I wasn't surprised. I didn't want to come back and this was my confirmation of that desire to stay, and of all I experienced that wonderful afternoon.

During our meditations we travel to many places. The first few months, we went often to Geoff's former home, to walk in the gardens. He enjoyed showing me around, however, in late autumn he became very frustrated at not being able to do anything there when he noticed something that had been overlooked, and these visits ceased until there is only the occasional one now. I always enjoyed the vibrations there which were very conducive to the meditative state. I also marvelled at the abundance of inspiration that created such beauty. This same inspiration is now being employed to create the gardens around Geoff's new home, and it isn't diminished at all. Although it is possible to create through thought, Geoff refuses to take any easy way and the choice is there to do it as he wishes, what he describes as the 'hands on' approach. My visits show me the projects unveiling a wealth of harmonious beauty and tranquillity.

Always with this book in mind, Geoff encouraged me early on to copy his designs onto graph paper. Unfortunately I am not artistic and one or two of my attempts have resulted in great mirth and merriment when he questioned exactly what it was I had depicted! However, I have done my best and will include some to show how alike it is to what we have here. This has always been our aim, to demonstrate the similarity and dispel the misconceptions that have been our understanding for so long. I have to stress however, my feeble attempts fall far short of the true beauty and colour, and can only give the merest impression. Also, Geoff has included features that make these designs suitable for recreation in this dimension.

This journey of discovery with Geoff hasn't always been easy. The whole contact has been far stronger than anything I have ever known before. My black state at the start meant I tried to deny frequently, and Geoff would not permit that. He made certain I was aware of his presence and heard what he had to say, always. Occasionally this caused friction and concerned Geoff quite a bit. He had no wish to add to my depressed state but equally, refused to be ignored. Now and then he felt he may have gone too far and I remember one occasion particularly. I had received a lecture over something I'd been stroppy over and it left me feeling low. During the evening I became aware Geoff was around. When I focussed on him, he showed himself dressed like a clown, and attempted to make me laugh, which succeeded fairly quickly.

On another occasion when he felt he had really upset me, everywhere I looked around the room, there were red roses. Every possible space held them and the scent wafted over me in waves. These were spiritual flowers of course, seen with the third eye, but the perfume is physically real. Scent is one of the easiest spiritual communications. I often have a sudden perfume fill the room, some I recognise, like freesias; which I am fond of, some are more elusive and keep me guessing. They are however, always very strong and undeniable.

There are a number of other regular places we visit in meditation, and these have become so familiar, I am sure if any of them are on earth, I would recognise them immediately should I ever come across them. However, some may well be on various astral planes, and by far my favourite place to visit is Geoff's home, and the wonderful gardens there. Earlier this year, he surprised me with a new garden he had created there, a private one he had designed around my favourite flowers and colours, where we could relax, meditate and talk. All the other areas are freely available for anyone to visit, both those in that dimension, and those here. This was always his aim, to provide a place to share with those seeking the peace and harmony of nature in beautiful surroundings; plus those from here who wish to surface their spiritual selves outside of their physical consciousness.

For the latter there is the Psychic Garden in spiritual colours of gold, purple and white. Other gardens reflect moods, the Pink Garden holds vibrations of love, a cottage style garden rambles in an abundance of colour and abandon, and presently underway, is a garden of water features where the sounds of water and birdsong mingle to create a vibration of life. I have done my best to give an accurate as possible idea of these but I am no artist and my efforts are way short of their true perfection.

During one of my visits to the gardens there, I noticed a cat wandering round. Geoff said she had been a family pet many years ago, and had found him again quite recently. I include this to show that our pets also have continuance and it may comfort those who grieve greatly for their companion animals, to know they can see them again one day.

The surroundings where Geoff lives, is mainly open countryside and I have seen sheep and horses in fields there. A lane runs past the house, no vehicles of course, as these are not needed to get around in dimensions where thought can do so much instantly. Now and then, people walk by just as they do here. Not far down the lane and across it, there is a footpath crossing the fields. Just off of this is a meadow of wonderful wildflowers, bordered by a hedge. At one end of this meadow is a magnificent silver birch, and the whole meadow has a golden glow and tremendous vibration of energy.

Some descriptions of these realms call them the lands of illusion which gives an impression they do not really exist but are the creation of those residing there, needing such normality before moving on to higher things. I am not certain if this is correct or not, but can only give my impressions. All I have seen there is definitely as real as this physical world. I go with an open mind and no set preconceptions, so I see what is there to see, not anything I expect to see. Many things come as a complete surprise therefore. Fortunately, not adhering to any religion, I am not swayed by the beliefs within those structures, and can observe it all in a more detached way. It is very beautiful and certainly a place I will be happy to find myself when finally leaving this physical world behind.

On Christmas Day 1997, I had a lovely surprise. The day itself has little significance in other dimensions. Those closer to earth know it is going on of course, and any who wish to join in, can find somewhere to do so. Not being religious, it is very much like any other day to me, and we were in fact, working on the book for part of it. However, during a lull in the severe weather, gales and rain, I took my usual walk around the garden and there, unscathed by the weather, was a red rose bud on the point of opening. I passed that way each day and knew it hadn't been there the day before! A cold snap earlier in the month had seen off any of the late roses. Having enjoyed its beauty for a couple of days, I decided to press the rose and keep it. Such gifts are worthy of their own continuance.

I still get many treats, unexpected and always welcome. To recall these in detail on waking, is such a joy. One recently was a concert which could only have been in the astral dimensions. A huge band stand, fringed behind by beautiful trees, held a full orchestra. Seats were arranged to the front, on grass. None of the music was familiar, I would describe it as light classical. But what made it special was every note played produced a corresponding colour in the sky above. This was nothing like laser light shows, but more akin to the old kaleidoscopes we looked into and turned to create coloured patterns. The patterns produced by the music were less defined, merging into each other to give a wonderfully gentle focus. Somehow it reached all the senses so the music and light could be felt within. I have no explanation for how this was achieved, the music and colours resonated with something deep within, to create a total experience which was both exhilarating, and very soothing.

A news item I found very upsetting not long ago, were the fires raging in Borneo, and the resulting effects on the Orang-Utan population. The sight of the tiny babies, such resignation on their faces, filled me with a desire to reach out to them with love and healing. I asked Geoff if we could go there for that purpose. We did so the same night and saw for ourselves, the horrifying destruction of the rain forest, another black mark on mankind. The sanctuary, we filled with light to aid their work. Some of the ape babies had terrible burns and it was sad to see them in that state. I cuddled one baby for ages, sending light and love out to surround him with those vibrations. It will be a very long time before I forget the sight of his face looking up at me, such trust in his liquid brown eyes. When will man learn the far reaching errors of his thoughtless destruction? We decided there was a need to continue sending out light and love to the sanctuary, and the rain forest. What will the apes who survive have to go back to?

Wonderful things are still happening; recently Geoff arranged a little gift for me. Every morning we link up by a stile down a footpath. I climb over this to feed the birds on a large flat stone. One morning, I reached the stile and found on the step, so neatly and accurately placed, a piece of coconut shell shaped like a shield. It was completely clean and so deliberately placed there. I picked it up and on the inside was my initial - J. Beneath this, the symbol of continuity, a sort of elongated figure eight on its side. I carry this around with me and will treasure it always. The significance of this lies in the product made from the outer waste of coconuts, Coir, something Geoff actively promoted when here.

Since that, I have received a couple more 'gifts'. One morning, as I placed my boots by the door ready to go out, I saw a stone right in the centre of the door mat. Immediately prior to this, the entire floor area had been swept, and the size of the stone meant it was impossible to miss. The door hadn't been opened either. I picked the stone up wondering how it could have got there. Then I noticed it was the shape of a triangle. I am very drawn to triangles although I have no idea why, and even have a metallic one I wear as a necklace. Turning the stone over, I saw something scratched onto the front face of it - a tiny L over an even tinier but perfect heart, and next to that, a large letter G.

The third gift 'arrived' in the back of a taxi to town on a wet summer day. When I got into the taxi there was nothing on the seat beside me. The next time I looked, a tiny silver coin sat there. The driver knew nothing of it so I popped it in my bag, and promptly forgot it. Two days later something urged me to take another look at it. I had thought it was a five pence piece but when I looked properly, it was an American one dime piece. On one side, around the profile of the relative president, was the word 'liberty'. This immediately struck a chord, just a few days before I had been talking to Geoff about the state of my life and how trapped I felt. This word suggested freedom.

The reverse of the coin carried an image of an eternal flame flanked by plants, one I recognised, oak. Then I looked at the year - 1994, the year of my hernia operation and my wonderings about death, also the year I lost my lovely dog, Shane. One small coin, but so many significant factors.

I suppose these gifts would be classed as 'apports'. However Geoff arranged them, I value them immensely. Nothing, however costly, could mean as much to me as these simple, but such thoughtful gifts; nor this contact and all it gives me, unmatchable by anything in the material world.

# Chapter Seven

# Geoff - Beliefs

How many times has something happened, something strange and unusual, which you have simply dismissed as imagination? Many people seek proof of an afterlife, but, conditioned to expect the kind of result achieved through years of scientific research, the events that can give you those proofs, are overlooked and dismissed as readily as brushing off a fly. How can you hope to gain knowledge of other dimensions when you seek them through physical means?

The answers lie within you, each and every one. You go around like automatons, taking on board whatever is dished out to you. You believe whatever you read in newspapers, and all that is told to you by 'experts'. You have lost the inclination to think for yourselves, because you have allowed yourselves to be controlled by others almost since the dawning of time.

The day will arrive when there is equipment capable of proving the existence of other dimensions. Many of the things proven today, were once doubted by sceptics. Once, material objects were thought to be solid, now it is recognised they are composed of atoms, and the force running through all things is energy, which is invisible.

Let's go back to my initial question and think about imagination for a moment. What is it? The process of imaging. Creating through thought. But in the density of the physical, it is faulty. Rarely do the things you imagine equal exactly what you create. Many factors come into this. Your imagination is limited, first by what you have actually experienced, not just in one life, but the period in between too. However, 'amnesia' of that time restricts you. Then, you are limited by what is fed you from birth, and out of that, what you take on as a belief.

Pause a moment to try a small exercise by way of demonstration. If I say picture in your mind a daisy. Almost everyone can do that easily even though if asked to draw that image, each picture would differ and no two would be identical. But supposing I said picture a flower from the planet Mercury? Some would say there are none! - How do you know? Others would picture something which would most likely resemble an earthly flower. Some would try to picture something but get nothing. But, those with more open minds may let a picture form in their minds and transcribe some flower quite unlike anything seen on earth. What would the reaction be to that? How many would say it was just their imagination? Would anyone consider the possibility of a correct image being placed in those minds by an unseen force? And if so, how many would laugh that idea down? Let's take that idea even further and ask, who could imagine some of those who saw a picture of a Mercurian flower, may have had a previous life on that planet? Maybe only one, who could then transmit that picture telepathically to the others? By now the hoots of derision are probably resounding off the ceiling. And here we have the crux of the matter - belief.

You are told there is no life on other planets, nor ever has been. Those who give you that information appear to speak from positions of authority, so you believe them. It doesn't even occur to the majority to question it. And it certainly doesn't occur to them to doubt it completely and ask for that knowledge to be given in some other way, for instance, by accessing that deep inner knowledge we all have within our subconscious. Or by receiving knowledge from a source in another dimension. Why? Because few believe in the latter anyway, again because of belief.

Have you ever stopped to consider this subject of beliefs and how they rule your lives? Most of us don't. We begin taking them on board as infants, listening to our parents and grandparents. If religion is on the agenda, we gain more of them there. Then comes school. By the time we reach the age of majority and begin the process of thinking for ourselves, most beliefs are firmly ingrained and will be so throughout our lives.

What we fail to understand is the nature of beliefs and just how they shape our lives and experiences. Their influence filters through everything, having an effect on all that you do.

The greatest gift any parent can give their children is to encourage them to have an open mind. But few do. Instead children are bombarded with all the beliefs parents took on when children themselves. Some of these are useful, but many are passed on without consideration of their continuing viability in changing times. As we evolve and progress, values change, but many old beliefs keep us in ignorance and under control.

Supposing I said to you almost everything you now believe and hold dear to be true, is faulty, misleading, or just downright wrong? That would shock you, wouldn't it, but it isn't that far off correct. Going back to the beginning of what we regard as 'civilised' living, we have been ruled by some authority or another. Those heading such authoritative bodies have a vested interest in preventing the remainder of us using our brains and thinking for ourselves. All the time we believe absolutely in what they tell us, we are kept in their control and in turn, they are kept in power. But, you will argue, without authority, there will be anarchy. It doesn't have to be so, there can be laws defining a difference between right and wrong. Thinking people will ascertain if those laws are fair or not, and if they are based on the Universal principle of cause and effect, karma, then it would be going some of the way to bringing balance to physical life.

Each of us perceives reality in a way unique to ourselves according to our conclusions on life, based on various ideas we have taken on board from those around us since birth. It is this nature of our personal reality, that which we see, hear, experience, during our formative years, where we draw the basic conclusions which form our beliefs. Reality as such, as it is regarded in physical terms, does not truly exist. When someone says be realistic, they really mean think as I do, see things as I do; or even, think as the masses do, see things as the masses do. But who has deemed the masses are correct? The Creator has not said this or that is impossible, this or that is absolute reality. It is mankind that states this or that is impossible.

Mankind interprets reality according to his or her conclusions about the very nature of reality. But each individual experience is different. Therefore no-one has any right to say my reality is totally correct and you must adhere to it. Individual reasoning in the physical dimension is not sufficiently aware to state categorically this or that is an absolute irrefutable certainty whether negative or positive. This applies no matter what seeming 'proof', or lack of it, might be presented by way of example. Those who present lack of evidence as 'proof', also do so according to their own conclusions about the nature of reality. They will therefore 'discover' their own 'proofs' that endorse that perception, proofs that often claim something is impossible because within their perception, that is the case. In fact, there is no such thing as impossible in terms of reality, only that a concept seems so because it has been that individual's lacking experience. Only by experiencing something does it then become possible, because there is nothing as conclusive as personal experience. Proof then, is largely indefinable in absolute terms. Rather than 'proof', it is better to seek inner knowing as your best guide. Inner knowing is absolute regardless of any outer definable 'proof'. Those with inner knowing need no proof, and inner knowing goes beyond belief. Those who doubt, and seek absolute proof, will never attain it, because for them, it won't exist; for them, no proof is possible. Conclude then, whatever you believe, based on your conclusions about your personal nature of reality, that will be your experience, created around you by your subconscious to fulfil your belief. If that ceases to provide you with a satisfactory life, then you will know you need to change your conclusions to alter beliefs, and it follows, your experiences will then change eventually too.

Some proclaim proudly they maintain a healthy scepticism. To do so means keeping your mind closed to possibility and how can that be classed as healthy? By far healthier is an open mind, one which accepts possibilities beyond all 'known' things, neither believing nor disbelieving until guided by intuitive knowing. This finds far greater scope within the creation of reality because of being totally open to all the endless and limitless wonders of possibility.

Obviously change is not going to happen overnight, and the most important factor for mankind, is the ability to question. But how many do? Sometimes it seems it is easier to sit back and take whatever is told to you as gospel. Apathy is the enemy of progress. What a different world it could be if each and every person on it, suspended all they believe to be true, and began again, looking at everything with a completely open mind and accepting the possibility of anything.

Why do you suppose scientific sceptics dismiss even the possibility of other dimensions? It isn't just because they cannot believe in anything apart from that they can see, touch, hear or measure. There are even those who offer huge rewards for proof, but that proof must satisfy scientists and that is impossible. Scientists are some of the most controlled beings on the planet. They are trained in controls. Their minds, for the most part; there are a few notable exceptions, operate along such narrow confines and boundaries, they are incapable of accessing anything any other way. And the reason scientists cannot come up with any proof is because they start off with a belief that there isn't any. Once a belief is in place, firmly lodged in your thinking, it takes a great deal of personal effort to shift it again.

Let me take another example here. There are two children of equal ability. One has chosen parents who believe in limitations and they constantly tell their child he must take whatever work he can find because people like them never amount to much. The other has chosen parents who believe in encouraging their child to do better than they did, and they constantly tell him he will be good at whatever he does. Which child do you think will grow up and make the more success of his life? Not only that, which do you think will be happier, more fulfilled. more content, and will attract like minded friends and companions to share his life? It is obvious really, isn't it. Putting aside any karmic challenges which include choosing our parents for whatever lessons we need, our conclusions about the basic beliefs we are fed while young, can have a bearing on our entire lives.

The example above is a blatant one but the majority of the beliefs that affect our lives are much more subtle and some have been going around for a very long time. I am referring now to the beliefs put out in the name of religion. These kind of beliefs are ones that won't only affect lives, but can affect you in between lives too.

All religions are basically the same and whatever name is given to the Source, the Creator; it is that Divine Supreme Power which is referred to. There is a lot of good within them when properly interpreted, but because that interpretation is left to the egoist nature of mankind, a great deal of harm has been done in the name of religion, and that is why that influence is now on the wane. The only real need for mankind to consider, is to have respect for the Divine Source, realise each of us is equal, all species have that Divine spark within, and do the best we can towards all things. If all people would develop a 'religion' of treating everything with respect, kindness, compassion, consideration, and unconditional love, just as they themselves would wish to be treated, living in harmony with all things, giving and taking in equal measure, that really is all that is asked of us.

There is no need for organised 'worship' with prayers and passages repeated by rote. The only prayers that reach beyond Earth, are the genuine ones from the heart and soul, giving thanks, or for help, and these are the ones acted upon. There is no credence here for all the rules and regulations created in the name of 'God' or whatever other name is used. These are purely applied to physical life and used to control through fear, limitation and restriction. They have no meaning here and some of them can make the transition into this dimension, and what you find here, very trying and difficult indeed, because you have taken in and believed that which was given by another physical being, interpreted and defined by that being's own limitations. How can one person in physical life, the densest level of existence, adequately claim to speak for the Creator of us all, and all of whom contain a spark of that Creator? Physical life is akin to school and we are all pupils. Our true teachers remain outside the physical dimension where they can operate free from the rigours of physical life. Sometimes they take an incarnation, to try and awaken us to the truth, but we are very slow to learn, even when given the wonders these incarnated higher beings can produce.

That has probably offended a lot of people which is regrettable, but it needs saying and thinking about if progress is to be continued. We are on the threshold of a new century, and a new age. This is a time when there has to be change, a rise in consciousness. It is vital for the survival of this planet. People must realise they are poisoning their world and harming themselves. New ways of living and relating have to be implemented. Personal responsibility must take over from victim mentality and blaming anything else. And to achieve this, we have to shake off all the beliefs that have held us back and prevented acceptance of our own personal role and responsibility in our own being.

One of the groups with much responsibility to herald change, are Spiritualists and all who come under that umbrella. It has to be said progress here is far too slow and there are no excuses, given the wealth of potential available. The problem lies within control again. The old guard are reluctant to alter tried and tested methods. There must be safeguards of course, but the days of darkened rooms and ectoplasm are long gone. The heirarchy in the spiritual movement tends to cling on to the old ways, and many mediums reflect this in still giving out the same old tired messages. A few now, being more open all round, are bringing through more advanced information and truths. This however, is not widely accepted or welcomed unfortunately. People now need educating in spiritual matters. They need to understand the way it all works to remove the confusions of life. Although a comfort in the early stages, it isn't really helpful long term, to give bereaved people the idea that their former loved ones will always be around them, watching over them, waiting for them etc. Does it never occur to anyone we have our lives to get on with, just as you do? There are those who do watch over each and everyone of you, guides and guardians, who are far better suited to that job. Even here, we all have the free will to choose. Many do, to start with, like to 'visit' family and friends even though warned it can be harrowing when there is no awareness of you being there. And for that reason, unless there is a specific purpose, those visits lessen as the reality of life here takes over. This is just as it should be, moving on to fulfil other purposes, both in the physical dimension, and in this one.

The new century will see more interaction between dimensions, more co-operation between worlds, growing acceptance and evidence that these other dimensions do exist in a different vibration. When this happens and it grows, as it will, eventually maybe leading to ways of providing absolute proof, then the majority of those outworn, outmoded beliefs will be shattered, to be replaced with beliefs born of truth and reason. Then it will resonate with the ancient knowledge we all have subconsciously, and physical life will become infinitely easier and understandable.

# Chapter Eight

# Other Lives

There is far more to each and every one of us than our present physical body. Unfortunately, teachings and other things we have been told for centuries, have led us to believe only in what we can see, hear and touch physically. This very narrow concept of life often results in enormous fear of dying, understandably, because we have forgotten our experiences of dying many times before. Such limited vision also makes us very selfish and arrogant. A belief in there 'only being one life', means we don't have to give much consideration to how we behave, and how we treat others and the world around us. We want it all and we want it now; live now before it is too late. That belief enables us to opt out of any personal responsibility because there will be no redress for our actions. Unfortunately this isn't correct and just like ignorance of the law is no defence, neither is ignorance of continuance, as many find out to their cost when passing over.

During the course of my contact with Geoff, I have had occasional flash backs to previous lives we have both taken part in. I have never had regressional hypnotherapy, in fact, I was once told I couldn't be hypnotised. Apparently a few people have some kind of built in resistance that makes them very poor subjects for hypnotism. Perhaps some of us with the kind of psychic abilities required for spiritual work need that protection to avoid any accusation of implanted suggestion? I like to think it ensures I am always in command of my faculties, and abilities.

The flash backs happen quite spontaneously. One moment I am here, maybe meditating or just talking with Geoff, and suddenly I am at the same time, both seeing and taking part in another lifetime. These are always very vivid and involve all senses. They won't be 'switched off' either, but must play out to the end, usually to the point of death each time. Although knowledge of the complete lifetime is there from the point of entry into it, it all plays out in just a few minutes.

I know once in spirit, we do review all our lifetimes. I am not sure why I have done so now, unless it is to be able to give reassurance to others about reincarnation and that death is something we all do many times and therefore, nothing to be feared or dreaded. Those who can accept death in this way, have a much easier time of passing. And those who have this understanding are surely more likely to live their lives doing their best for themselves and others, harming none or what is around them.

So far, I have surfaced seven other lifetimes. None of them very remarkable but it is possible to see patterns of learning emerging through them. There have been various relationships, brother and sister in the early seventeen hundreds, father and daughter in China at the time of the Mongol invasions, and many others. What is so remarkable is the recognition. No matter what physical 'shell' we are wearing, somehow there is an inner something that knows as soon as there is eye contact. I cannot define it because it goes beyond anything understandable in physical terms. I suppose the nearest equivalent is when meeting a complete stranger for the first time, and knowing somewhere you have known them before. Somewhere deep inside there is instant recognition of something within that other person. Logically, it can only be a soul recognition, and that in itself, opens up amazing possibilities way beyond the limited ideas of the physical dimension.

I have also been told of yet further other lifetimes seen by others with the ability to see such things. One of these, that Geoff and I were together attending one of the mystery schools in ancient Egypt.

There have of course, been lifetimes apart too. Geoff told me recently, since he has been in that dimension and reviewing lifetimes, he has discovered one where a family member in this lifetime, played a role as his mother in a previous one. And in that former life, he was female and born disabled. At that time his 'mother' could not accept or cope with it, reducing him to little more than a servant while she got on with the pleasures of life. Mercifully, it wasn't a long life for him, ending around twenty, but this lifetime gave opportunity for the karmic debts and lessons not learned then, to be balanced, worked out and released now.

This example gives a clear indication of how physical life is not the reality we perceive it to be, and why we should always do our best in it because, to quote a well known saying: what goes around, comes around. We escape nothing, get away with nothing, however clever we think we have been, and any harm we do to others, not just humans either, is a debt that must be paid back sometime, with interest.

We probably all have to reach a certain level of evolution/ progression before we permit ourselves memories of the next dimension. Some of our lifetimes are very hard indeed, and if we had this knowledge at that stage, it would be easy to cut short the incarnation and renege on whatever we were intended to do. This could have tremendous repercussions, not only for ourselves, but for those interacting with us, thus creating horrendous karma to be worked out. It is mainly for this reason that we have such 'amnesia' while in physical life.

One question I have been asked on this, is how do we know when something we are doing is not repaying bad karma done previously to us? The answer is intuition. We all have a higher self which in part, gives us our small voice of conscience. Many deny, but really, we all know when something is right or wrong. It is a basic faculty and if we follow our inner feelings, going with what feels right always, then we cannot make mistakes. Sometimes, following the right course means having to be cruel to be kind. Those are difficult lessons but recognised as such in spiritual terms. We can be sure when tackling and completing those lessons successfully, our progression will be that much advanced. And if doubts confuse, then ask for guidance. We all have access to that but we do have to ask before it can be given.

I have always had a belief in reincarnation but my ideas on this were a bit woolly previously. For instance, I cherished a notion that those who enjoyed hunting animals, and those who experimented on animals etc., might come back as those creatures to experience exactly what it felt like. Learning by example. Now I understand that we humans evolve through the various life forms, including animals, and we cannot go back to a former life form. But those participating in such practices I am told, will learn the errors of their ways, and it will be an even harder lesson than my simplistic notion. We abuse others at our peril!

Many people however, love and respect animals, and another frequently asked question is whether animals survive? Some creeds deny animals a soul! What a strange idea showing so obviously how mankind gets things wrong. As animals eventually evolve into humans, of course they have a soul and survive.

Sometimes we come across an animal, maybe a pet, with whom we seem to have a special bond. I believe when this happens that soul is one of our group, or of a linked group, close to the point of becoming human. We do not after all, progress at an equal rate. Where something is required through that bond, it cannot be broken until the intention completed, and I have a personal example of this.

In 1991, I took in and cared for two goats. Their owner was moving and the new house had no space for them. The arrangement was supposed to be for just a few months until an alternative was found. As the months went on, the owner wanted the goats to have kids and seeing this as an opportunity to expand my knowledge, also being very fond of goats, I agreed. The goats were duly mated and eventually the time came for them to give birth. The first goat had twins with the owner present, one of each sex. A month later, the second goat showed signs of imminent birth. Goats are highly intelligent ruminants and not only enjoy human company, but at times like kidding, actually want human company.

After a lot of straining it became obvious the second goat had some problem. Often, the kid's front legs will be in the wrong position and this was the case here, requiring me to act as 'midwife', actually easing the tiny creature into the world. It was an unforgettable moment, and right from that point I was aware of having a special bond with that kid. He turned out to be the first of triplets, the other two being female. As he grew that bond developed, but the owner had no interest in keeping males and insisted he, along with the male kid from the first goat, would be going for slaughter at a few months of age. No amount of arguing would persuade him, not even offering to buy him despite being the goats' carer anyway! He was just five months of age when the owner collected and took him away, and it broke my heart.

Seven months after this incident, a complete stranger pulled up and knocked on my door. This happens from time to time, someone will turn up with something 'wild' in need of help. On this occasion it was a gentleman saying he had found a baby owl that had 'fallen' out of its nest. This turned out to be a baby tawny, just a week or so old. Tawnys leave the nest

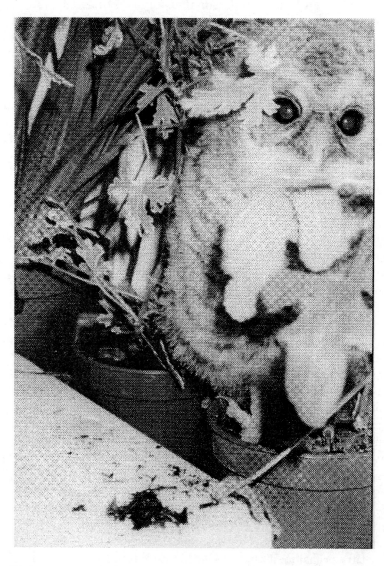

Wol, our resident tawny owl, as a baby. First ventures into gardening!

quite early and wander around at the foot of their trees, often causing well meaning people to think they have been abandoned. Once removed however, it would have been risky to try and replace him so I would have to rear him. Owls are a particular favourite of mine and this one was an amazing character. It didn't take very long before I began to see things that reminded me of my little goat kid. It is difficult to explain how an owl can appear to have similar traits but to start with, it was something in his expression when I spoke to him. I had a growing feeling that my little goat kid had come back to me, reincarnated as a tawny owl. What clinched it for me was when I said to the owl; 'Are you him? Have you come back?' He was just beginning to fly and liked to sit on my shoulder. At my question, he flew onto to a shelf where I had a photo of my little goat kid, stopping right in front of it and glancing from me to the photo and back again. This happened twice more and convinced me. Once I accepted this possibility, he reverted to being, and growing, as an owl. He is still with me as he became too imprinted for survival in the wild, and yes, there is a special bond between us too. Not only is he extremely affectionate, indeed this was a characteristic of my little goat kid too, but he also 'talks' to me in a quite remarkable variety of different sounds.

Whenever anything appears in the media concerning reincarnation, there are those who have to spring forward eagerly with denials. Most of these 'experts' trot out their theories by way of 'reasoned' explanation. It is just this kind of opposing view, on this subject and many others in this field, that has held back advances through belief systems. Just like a tug of war, it shuffles this way and that, not really gaining ground either way. Those brave enough to speak out about their experiences are made to feel they have some kind of mental problem, or it is all their imagination. How arrogant these 'experts' can be. Those experiencing don't say; 'I am right, you must believe me', they are just so overjoyed to have that experience, they rightly want to share it, so others may

Wol in 2001

find their own. They tell their tales and leave it to those able to believe, to do so. Yet the 'experts' proclaim, advocate, and pontificate. They always come across with an attitude of knowing best, knowing it all. But by the very nature of their complete denial, they cannot have those experiences, therefore cannot know it all. I feel it is very wrong and very negative of these people to express their views so forcibly, sometimes in doing so, destroying an element of hope in others. They are entitled to their opinions, however they gain them, but not to inflict their doubts on others with seeming 'authority'.

I have encountered people with genuine experiences, thoroughly distressed by such 'experts', because being new to them, have been made to feel they are going mad or similar. What harm is done to others in that way; and in what can only be classed as intolerance, that same negative force that creates racial, class, religious, and other unrests. When all can accept others without seeking to interfere in their chosen lives, harmoniously trusting that all are where they should be in the course of evolving, then this world will truly be ready to take its rightful place in our Universe.

# Chapter Nine

# Geoff - Recognise the Magic in Your Life

Whatever kind of life you have, and as we have established this is largely governed by karma, as well as the need to learn and experience, every life contains elements of magic. By magic, I mean of course, that Divine spark each of us has inside. And it is that spark that puts a touch of magic into physical life, even the dreariest.

Once you recognise and accept you have that spark, that magic, life becomes less of a struggle and a burden, and things open up in ways that surprise, even seeming miraculous at times. You will find aspects of synchronicity in so many areas. What once was dismissed as coincidence, takes on a whole new meaning, and leads you to finding yourself led along pathways of discovery rich with meaning.

Every day can be a wonderful new experience, a joy to behold. Imagine waking each morning and welcoming whatever the day throws at you! Seeing purpose in everything and accepting it wholeheartedly. When you can recognise the spiritual side of mankind, and see the Divine workings filtering through everything, you can embrace life with a sense of responsibility, and when you do that, the magic will really work for you.

One of the areas we find difficult to understand while physical, is in getting back what we give out. This is an immutable law in cosmic terms. The basis of karma. It works so simply - when we think or do bad things towards another, that 'badness' will return to us. Equally, when we think nice thoughts and do good deeds, that also will return to us, and how much better to be on the receiving end of nice things! Now and then we see an example of someone for whom life flows, everything goes their way, and they get on well with everyone. Although some of that may be 'good' karma, there is no reason why all shouldn't emulate that so that even the necessary challenges assume an easier role. All it takes is having a different outlook on life and an unconditional acceptance of other people, recognising that while we may not agree with others' opinions, life style etc., and are free to express our own views since we all learn from each other, we can never force others against their own free will, nor should we attempt to do so.

It is impossible to like every person you meet. Some wind us up because their attitudes don't fit in with ours. That is natural, but why let it affect you to the extent you start feeling hatred and loathing, and worse, wishing something dire would befall them. Isn't it better to accept you are not going to get on with certain people and put distance between you? That isn't so easy of course, if such people happen to be in a working or family environment. Avoidance where possible, is the best way, but you can still distance yourself in any encounters. And while you may not actually be able to feel love, however detached, towards them, you can surely at least visualise them surrounded in light. This has two results, to prevent them actually causing you upset; and, you will receive much better things back for your efforts. By far preferable to all the conflict and strife that is the lot of so many, causing additional stress. If nothing else, smile at people you know dislike you. It will confuse them, and you will feel better for it!

Far too many people seem hell bent on forcing others to accept their personal viewpoint on a number of issues. There is no problem with reasoned debate, that is a way of learning, but it is very wrong to attempt any forcing of opinions on others. This is the nature of control and has been practised by those in authority for far too long. To take one example, an emotive issue like abortion. As with any emotive issue there are those adamantly for, and in equal measure, those against. Nothing wrong with that as we all have free will and at various stages in the course of evolvement, will have opinions on such things. But that doesn't give us any right to think our opinion is the correct one, forcing others to adopt it. In spiritual terms there is no judgement either way.

Such things are understood and the reasons for them, there is always purpose involved and choices for those in that position. I don't intend to go through a list of possible purposes, each individual has their own way of learning. But those who are against, have no right whatsoever to attempt to inflict their will on others, or seek to exert control over them in that process. They are quite entitled to think and believe as they do, but not to impose their will on those who think and believe differently. The most likely immediate result will be anger, and anger, as I have demonstrated elsewhere, is always at ourselves whatever the denials of that, and as such, is a very self destructive energy. In some cases, the anger will be because on an inner level, it is known that it is wrong to try and influence others against their will when the best way is to accept unconditionally, a different choice. Neither can say which is right, because there is no right or wrong. Nor can it be classed as protecting the unborn because that being also has choice and would be there for just that purpose. To deny another their learning or karmic experience is a serious error and one that will require balancing eventually.

Another example is that of suicide. Many taking that exit route attempt to place the blame for it on others. The classic thinking is of being 'driven' to it by someone or something. That 'excuse' has no credence once in this dimension. Always, always, there is personal responsibility and those whom the suicide attempts to blame, are his/her own attractions for the purpose of learning. Challenges which have been agreed in advance and this is why any suicide used as an 'opting out' is regarded as wrong. Not that it is judged any more than any other mistake. The judging is done by each individual upon themselves and the knowledge of having to face those challenges again in another lifetime, is a formidable lesson. More so, the knowledge that any enforced guilt left on another, will also have to be resolved.

All of these mistakes cause negative energies which remain within the consciousness of the soul, usually becoming subconscious upon reincarnation yet affecting that being until they are dealt with and released or transmuted. The same is true of positive energies but these bring positive creations into the reality of that being, and this is why various things are attributed to a 'good' or 'bad' start in life.

There is so much more behind each physical life experience, known only to that individual at a deeper level, and this is why no-one has any right to judge another or attempt to exert control over them. And this applies whatever the relationship. Parents may guide according to their beliefs, but must not force their children against their own choices. And nobody should go against their own will for the sake of pleasing another if it feels uncomfortable to do so. To live your life pleasing another's will is, in effect, taking responsibility for that person, and the only one you must assume responsibility for in any lifetime, is yourself. You may argue you do things to please others out of love. Of course there are times for give and take within relationships, putting aside selfish needs to meet someone halfway. But that is different to allowing your whole life to revolve around someone else's wishes to the exclusion of your own choices.

There are only two certainties in life - you are born, and; you will die. In between, your life will be as you create it, attracting to you all you need to learn lessons, sort out karmic debts, meet your challenges, or just experience. So why not enjoy all of that by adding that touch of magic to it? Make no mistake, there are no hapless 'victims', or 'accidents'. Fate is mankind's excuse for 'unexpected' good events, or bad. But all events are pre-arranged by you and by any who agree to co-learn etc., with you. Once you grasp that, you can take command of your own life and create it as you wish, not as something tossed this way and that by the random creations of your subconscious.

This is how it happens when you allow yourself to think in terms of something 'out there' pulling the strings. There is no puppet-master. You have the Divine spark within you and that spark is all you need to live your physical life in a magical way. Yes, you still have to do the learning, but it isn't a punishment however hard it seems. In fact, it is often because of that random creation of your subconscious that it works out much harder than it need, because your sub-conscious cannot reason, and like some advanced computer, pulls out files from many lives to back up its selection of events for you.

Don't doubt your ability to achieve this. Each doubt is like a barrier you erect in front of you, preventing you seeing the light. Just bear in mind always, the more you give/devote to pursuing more spiritual aims over material ones, and the more you seek spiritual knowledge to make sense of life, the more you will receive, and this includes evidence, although this largely, cannot be identified in physical terms. It is the inner knowing which cannot dismiss it, or the magic that flows through your life with joyful abandon.

The magic you find in your physical life doesn't end when you leave that life. In fact, the more you find it while incarnate, the easier it is to adjust to life in the spiritual realms. There is abundant magic here once free from the limitations carried through from physical life.

Do you ever wonder why we can take nothing tangible from the physical world, with us when we die? Many have attempted to do so, but all have failed. It is for the same reason we are prevented from taking our physical body with us - vibration. Things created in the physical world operate at a different vibration to the etheric dimensions. In the same way, when we eventually leave the etheric levels and move on to the higher dimensions, we again have to leave behind all we have created that operates at the correct vibrational frequency for these levels. This is all worked out with Divine perfection and that same perfection means we don't actually have to do without anything of real meaning to us. We can re-create whatever we like here, and often find exact facsimiles already waiting for us. This is because tangible things we feel most strongly for, created by our thoughts and emotions, actually manifest in these realms first, before doing so in the denser vibration of physical life. And that is magical!

Taking command of your physical life, accepting totally, personal responsibility for all that you experience and acting accordingly, is liberating. No-one can control you or even influence you against your will. All too often that is exactly what happens until individuals feel helpless and unable to cope. Only you can give away your power to others by allowing them to influence your life. Take back your power and find the magic that can make your life work so well. What are seen as 'bad' things will still happen but understanding the purposes, or even just accepting there is a purpose for all things, can reduce their ability to devastate you. It isn't what happens to you in life that really matters, but how you deal with it, how you react to it. You can go under, or you can move on and overcome all things. Only when you have no belief in continuance, does life seem so daunting. It can't be stressed enough, life and all that is physical passes into oblivion; you will not. You go on eternally, an essential being that cannot be destroyed.

Each earthly day is like a micro-experience of life and death. Each morning you wake refreshed, anew, (reborn). Events of the previous day, even traumatic ones, have faded. You start each new day with hopes, expectations, and aims. The day ahead is a new sheet waiting to be filled. As the day progresses, you achieve these, or not, depending upon various factors.

In the morning you are lighter, more energetic. During the course of the day you slow down gradually, feel heavier, and by late evening you feel tired, unable to think so clearly, and are ready for sleep. While sleeping you are free. Your sleep-time experiences, however you define them, whether in the form of dreams or more, free you entirely. There are no limits or restrictions. You travel and create with ease. You have all kinds of experiences which mostly, you have control over. You can go where you wish, meet whoever you wish, and can do whatever you wish. How often do you wake with the memory of a lovely 'dream' and would dearly like to be back in it? This then is the very essence of life, death, progress and evolution, all wrapped up in a brief twenty-four hour period. And when you finally leave the physical world, you will look back on your many other lifetimes in the same way, as brief, as varied, and as complete as each of your days are now.

Making each day count as much as each lifetime, with the same importance and emphasis on doing your best, releases that Divine magic to flow for you. Life becomes a joyous experience, and you will find an expression of joy in every day. You can do it. It is one reason why you chose to incarnate, and when eventually you get it right, physical life will truly become an example of 'Heaven' on Earth.

# Chapter Ten

# Into The Future

This book has been very enjoyable to do, and I hope some may find enjoyment in it, as well as hopeful and useful information. Although I have had some remarkable experiences, and a lot of evidence, some of which actually tangible, there would be nothing to satisfy any scientist by way of 'proof'. I can only say I tested as much as possible, all along the way, challenging Geoff to give me the confirmations I required to convince me. It was important to me that all I experienced was the truth, and thankfully, Geoff was as keen on that too, willing to provide as much as possible, that which I would accept as evidence. I have no doubts because I have a total inner knowing. This is not something that can be measured, or seen, and it would mean nothing to anyone else because we all have to seek and find such things in the way which is right for us. No two people will have exactly the same experiences, the vastness of it all ensures that. Therefore, each account can only be given from that person's perspective, but there may well be something within such pages which strikes a familiar note within you, and leads you to seek further, following this pathway of wondrous discoveries and happenings.

Although very satisfying and giving a sense of fulfilment, there is also something a little sad in completing a book, a finality in the culmination of many months of working in harmony to produce this work. And what comes after it? I would like to think there may be other books, and Geoff will wish to continue to write. I have certainly indicated my willingness for any such future project. Things are happening so quickly now, that some information is almost out of date by the time it is published. Those in the physical dimension will need guidance during the process of change, but eventually, I believe everyone will awaken and have their own link in spirit, so will receive personal guidance.

We will certainly continue with our rescue work while there is a need for this. Maybe the time will come when even this work changes in the course of natural progression. As we all raise our vibrations and have greater links with other dimensions we will not be so confused about our roles and why we are here, or about life and death, and each will follow the other as normally as night now follows day. Until then, there are still many souls lost, confused, needing help to be guided to the light or simply persuaded of what has happened to them.

I personally have no fears concerning death, and I feel fortunate in knowing all that awaits me there. I am very glad that my awareness and consciousness have been awakened enough to allow me the glimpses I have had. It is my intention to enjoy every moment between lives, free of the restrictions and limits imposed on us here, also to add to my knowledge as much as possible. I am sure there will be a further incarnation, one shared together, because of unfinished purposes which cannot be achieved in that dimension, and when that comes about, it will be without the 'amnesia' now accompanying most physical experience. This 'amnesia' giving us the veils between us and other dimensions, so necessary where karmic lessons are required, but also causing the doubts about all continuance. How much better when we can enjoy a lifetime in full awareness of our spiritual selves, everything working in harmony.

One of the most hopeful things I have learned, is that while we might have ambitions which may never be fulfilled here, they can all do so in the next dimension. Doesn't that make more sense of life? What point would there be to it if those who's experiences were hard from birth to death, those who's entire lives are marked with unhappiness, pain and suffering could never know anything else? There would be a certain degree of cruelty in such a scenario, something many would happily attribute to 'God's will' - just as long as it wasn't their experience! And it is mankind's muddled lack of understanding about personal responsibility that makes him look always, for blame elsewhere. How much better to know it is our lessons, which, if completed satisfactorily mean all things, all heartfelt desires, can be achieved, realised in the afterlife as required. Divine perfection that gives such flow and purpose to everything. It was once said, the saddest words uttered at the end of life are 'if only'. Not any more with this knowledge those words can be changed to; 'now that is over, I can in truth, begin living'. The simple message repeated for many years now, has been, nothing is impossible. If we can free ourselves from the imposed restrictions and limited thinking that has controlled us all for so long, what a wonderful future awaits us. A future without fear; knowing peace, joy and happiness really is our destiny, both in this dimension, and all the others to follow.

And what about Earth, what of the future there? Many predictions are being suggested at the moment. These range from real gloom and doom facing us all to a rise in vibration all over. There can be little doubt that change is needed and long overdue. We are poisoning our world; the land, the seas, even the air. What kind of mentality decreed it was o.k. to pour raw sewage into the sea? Even worse, to allow radio active waste to be disposed of, dumped there too? I cannot believe the risks were unknown, but no doubt financial considerations overruled common sense. The resulting problems in marine life may be the least of our worries. Who knows what horrific mutations could be waiting in the wings to be launched onto an unsuspecting populace?

Yet despite the evidence of these and other abuses on our world, man complacently sits back and waits. We each have a duty to care for the planet which is home to us for our physical sojourns.We neglect that duty at our peril, the penalties could be enormous.Those who govern have greatest responsibility but each one of us can do our best too. The day could just be close when nature throws in the towel and then what can we say to our children and grandchildren when they ask, why didn't you heed the warnings before it was too late?

Sometimes when I look around and see the atrocities still going on, the selfish way some treat their own kind let alone other life forms I wonder if a rise in consciousness is possible on a mass scale. I have to trust that it is achievable, and that a better life and world will result. I may not even be in this dimension then but I will certainly view it all with interest from beyond. If in some small way, our words here can contribute towards that better world, then I will feel I have achieved something worthwhile from this incarnation.

Geoff and I have discussed many times the state and condition of this planet, and how things may change. We often talk idealistically too, about the way we would like to see things unfolding as the new century begins. Although questioned several times by friends about the various current predictions, he has no definite knowledge and always replies that nothing is cast in concrete because it depends on many factors not least, the reactions of people, and how quickly they awaken and take responsibility for what they are doing. Some of course, already do so and make valiant attempts but they are too few in numbers to make a significant difference.

Although Geoff may not have specific details to impart to us on major planetary changes there are a number of projects he is involved in, which will eventually manifest in the physical world. He will not allow me to reveal precise details of this work except to say some projects are linked to conserving nature, and others, concerned with plant welfare. I find this work tremendously exciting and feel privileged to have this understanding of the co-operation that exists between the dimensions. Few may realise the extent to which this goes on, and those who believe the physical is the only world, miss out on so much. The expression 'as above, so below', adequately sums up how new discoveries, inventions, and a whole host of other things, begin their creation in spirit before eventually manifesting in physical forms. Unfortunately mankind often perverts the wonderful knowledge received in this way, and grotesque counterparts result. However, as we move into the new millennium, this between worlds co-operation will not only grow, but we will all become more aware of it and realise the responsibility we must all exercise within the boundaries of free will. Our world can become Heaven on Earth in every way, if we can all overcome the negative side of our nature.

Now and then major events shake this world causing a mass solidarity that inspires; or we see mass enthusiasm and energy pouring out in support for a sports event, rock concert, or something similar. If those same mass qualities were utilised in demanding something be done to sort out and heal this planet, no authority could stand against that, and what a difference it would make. But sadly, for the most part, mass apathy is all that rouses when planetary needs are raised.

Mankind strives to live forever through the use of cryogenics. I have never been able to understand this because we all live forever anyway. The possible horrific consequences of this would frighten me far more than death ever could. The only winners can surely be those who make huge sums of money out of this, feeding on the fears of those who dread death, believing there is no afterlife, no continuance.

I haven't seen any discussion of what the result of cryogenics would be on the spirit. Should physical bodies ever be successfully resuscitated, would the spirit be forced back in again? Or would that being then end up a soulless zombie? Maybe any wandering spirit could take over the body, claiming it as its own. Perhaps it has never been discussed because there is no realistic prospect of resuscitation once the physical vehicle has been exited.

Whatever may or may not occur as we approach the millennium and move into a new century, I do know I will go on sharing fascinating conversations and experiences with Geoff. Our talks over these past two years have expanded my knowledge enormously and I look forward to that continuing. I feel I have grown a lot too. Geoff has given me such courage and confidence, with his support and help, among other things, I have been able to speak out about events which have over-shadowed and affected my life since my childhood, thus clearing karmic challenges and healing in the process. Something very necessary for me to achieve before my own transition.

I have no conscious knowledge of when that transition will be, but ever since my teens, I have had an inner feeling this wouldn't be a very long incarnation. This doesn't bother me at all. When that time arrives I will greet it joyously, with a sense of excitement, and an anticipation of the new life that awaits me. I have even planned to the last detail my finale from this world. It is very important to me that it is done exactly as I wish, not as others think it should be. My choice therefore, is no religious ritual whatsoever, but a beautiful Pagan/Shamanic ceremony with words and music that have real personal meaning. I see this as an act of responsibility over something which in every life, is inevitable. And having seen my plan which is also ecologically friendly in every way, some of my family and friends are also now opting for something similar.

Meanwhile I will go on doing my best for this world, giving service in the way that has manifested for me. In doing so, maybe it is allowing Geoff an element of living on through me and with me, working together in our efforts to help create a better physical world.

# Chapter Eleven

# Geoff - Changes

Planet Earth is on the brink of catastrophe and its population is complacently sitting back refusing to acknowledge what is happening. There is a limit to the amount of beings a world can sustain. It is no different to fleas on a cat, too many will take too much and the host will die.

In order to sustain the ever growing population, methods have been developed for ever more intensive farming. Included in this comes mass spraying of crops to destroy pests, and spraying of the ground to destroy weeds. Then there are artificial booster fertilisers; nitrates in abundance, some of which leak into rivers polluting them and killing fish.

All these 'additives' are designed to produce the biggest 'healthiest' yield possible to satisfy ever growing demand. Livestock doesn't escape either, pumped full of antibiotics and growth enhancers to get more meat out of each animal, more milk out of each cow and so on. Even that isn't enough so they mess about with genes, resulting in livestock that cannot adequately even manage to give birth without help. And as if all that wasn't enough of messing with nature, someone decided cloning would be a great idea to produce even more!

Dealing with all the waste produced by so many requires a massive unhealthy cocktail of chemicals. Industry goes flat out on production levels, and pollution is on a grand scale as a result. All of these and more pours harmful substances on and into the planet starting a cycle of destruction which is now very close to critical.

Every living thing, animate or inanimate, has an aura. Those who can read them can tell the state of the being from the colour vibrations within their aura. Viewing that aura from these and other dimensions shows the exact state of the planet, which also has its own aura. The colours range the entire spectrum from white the highest and purest, to black, which shows the most serious harm. At the moment, there is an awful lot of black!

Can there be any on Earth who do not believe drastic changes are vital to the survival of Earth and all its inhabitants? Amazingly - sadly - yes! And many of them hold positions that would enable them to create such changes, if only they would wake up and take notice.

The message to them is simple - get out of your apathetic, complacent ruts and start seeing the truth. Do something now. Not next month, next year, sometime, never. This issue is not going to go away. It is going to get worse, and worse, and worse.Have you learned nothing from BSE and similar examples?

It causes much frustration - yes, we do still have such feelings here to see and understand all that is going on; the covert operations; the hidden agendas; the cover ups. Mostly done in the name of commerce and industry, for which you can read 'greed'. But if those in positions of power, authority, won't take heed, then maybe these words will reach enough of the population to cause them to rise up and demand change now. You elect the politicians to serve you and do their best for your interests, not their own. It is your world, and an amazingly beautiful one. Do you want to see it destroyed? Do you want to see your children and grandchildren born with disease and deformities caused by pollutants? Doesn't the ever growing incidence of asthma and respiratory illness' worry you at all? (I speak of these in earthly terms without considering the spiritual implications. Your children are trying to persuade you to wake up by showing what is happening now!) Do you want to exist without hope?

Mankind has created the monster, the problems, and only mankind can solve them. Not the fish in the dying seas. All they can do is demonstrate what you are doing wrong. Not the creatures who live on the land and fly in the air. All they can do is reflect the problems back where they came from. Not the plants and the trees, most of which are screaming out for help but go unheard. We, now in this dimension, cannot do it for you. We help where we can, and channel healing and light where it is most needed, but it is a losing battle until mankind finally wakes up to his errors and his responsibility to his world. Only mankind can remedy the root causes. Do it now, before it is too late. Stop immediately all dumping in the seas of anything that isn't naturally occurring there. You have no true idea of what is happening, right now, and to pour toxic substances into the oceans is an atrocity and one for which, there are no excuses. Stop producing chemicals that harm. Stop manufacturing anything that damages any part of the environment. Stop all nuclear testing, it is madness and the harmful results will reverberate out across huge areas. And stop right now, all genetic modifications. This alone is an ultimate nightmare waiting to be unleashed on all sentient life.

Even if all this is achieved right away, it will still take a very long time and require a lot of work, both on Earth, and from these dimensions, to restore all balances. There is no leeway for reductions over periods of time. You no longer have that luxury. Act now, or cause untold suffering on your world and those living on it. The consequences will be yours, and yours alone. You cannot escape Divine justice, whether you believe in it or not.

114

If - and at the moment it by no means certain, adjustments are made to sort out the wrongs being heaped on the planet, what can be expected as we move into a new century? Many things will occur to ensure the natural course of evolution in the unending Universal flow. Some of these changes are already happening and have been doing so gradually for around thirty years or so. But now, all things are speeding up.

All will be raising their vibrations in the next few years and in doing so, you will be able to gain awareness of the spiritual dimensions and those in spirit, because your vibrations will then be on a par with ours. So many deny their spiritual side and all idea of continuance. Unfortunately those who ought to be promoting open and seeking minds, are the worst culprits. The media in general tends to fall down on the cynical side. Journalists, by the very nature of their work, seeing a lot of 'life' from all angles and every aspect, take a lot of convincing. Also, there is a growing trend now in the light of competition, for newspapers etc, to print anything whether strictly accurate or not, even altering what is said in interviews, or twisting facts, to produce something more 'sensational'. This element of deceit effects those perpetrating it, and by reflection, they will regard all things they cannot prove or fully understand, as illusions or impossible. Dismissing it all as easily as they dismiss their duty to report truthfully.

Along with vibrations, there will also be a rise in consciousness. It is this that will awaken. You will all find a growing awareness that you have a spiritual side, that there is something that goes far beyond all that you regard as reality. For most, the physical reality which has served them adequately for so long, will begin to pall. It will no longer be enough to provide a meaning to life. Some of you are finding this already. Life seems to lack purpose, incentive, or inspiration. There is an underlying need for fulfilment which nothing in your present reality can satisfy.

Consciousness is a strange thing. Mostly we are ignorant of it existing beyond it making a statement as to who and where we are. In that, we tend to ignore the other information it attempts to provide for us, such as the greater awareness. All too readily we accept the words of those who insist the physical is the only reality. As this universal rise in consciousness manifests over a period of time, some will get there faster than others, those who have gone beyond the basic concept of consciousness. The physical reality accepted until now, will fade, bringing more spiritual values forward. Living within a more spiritual reality will become common-place, and only by working with those in spirit, and in that reality, will you find life fulfilling and satisfying. In fact, the only real flow to life will lie on that pathway. Undoubtedly there will be resistance as those who have adamantly proclaimed against continuance find their reality turned upside-down. Things will happen that force them to think again, and possibly, rethink all they have believed to date. Many will find what worked before, no longer does so, and they will have to change the patterns to find new answers, shifting paradigms to make sense of all that is going on around them. For a hardened few, it will really be a rebirthing process, learning from scratch again.

There is already a learning process going on at the present time. Before vibrations can be lifted, there is a need to resolve karma. That, you will remember, is the law of cause and effect. Every action, every thought, every deed you do, creates a ripple, a cause, and for each and every one there will be an effect. For centuries, good and bad deeds could be held over from one lifetime to another, even a future lifetime if desired. This may be why you experience events in this lifetime that make you wonder what you have done to deserve it! You will find out when you leave the physical dimension. Now however, there is the need to clear this balancing of things much quicker in preparation for the vibration and conscious-ness rise. Negative karma in particular, cannot be carried along with that rise and must be cleared first. What you will be experiencing are elements of instant karma. This means any bad actions, thoughts or deeds will bring almost instant effects, circling back on the perpetrators and causing them many problems until they learn to go about things differently, deal with things in a better, more acceptable way. Good actions, thoughts and deeds will also bring instant effects too of course, but it is the negative side that needs subduing to bring about the next stage in mankind's evolution.

In this chapter I have been more serious than entertaining. This is deliberate because the subject matter needs addressing now. But I will close it on an important lighter note. There is nothing you cannot achieve through love because love is the most vital ingredient of all. Love is the one thing prevalent throughout the Universe and all life. It really is love that keeps it all going, and love of all kinds is why we incarnate, to discover love and experience its many forms. Love created us, and love gave us free will to go out and follow our own paths, find our own way through the many rich and colourful levels of life's experiences. And love truly can overcome all things, even the most negative, but there is Divine order even in that.

First learn to love yourself. That is essential if you are ever to truly express love for others, and maybe that is why it is the most difficult aspect of all. Learn to love and accept where you may lack perfection, and you can then unconditionally accept imperfection in others and love them regardless too. Once you honestly love yourself, warts and all, then you are ready for that significant other, and the true eternal love that exists in that unending bond. In that union, you can radiate love out selflessly to others and the world - spreading a philosophy of love wherever you go. It hasn't happened too much so far, just now and then shining examples surface of just what heights can be reached. That too is now changing as more and more clear their karmic debts. When eventually all can achieve this, it will become Heaven on Earth, and even more things will become possible. Real love is for eternity and knows no boundaries limits or restrictions. And that's what life and evolution is all about, operating through the positive vibration of love and harmony in the New Age, taking our rightful place in the Cosmos, and leaving behind the negativity which has overshadowed and controlled us for so long.

# Chapter Twelve

# Geoff - Information

During the course of our contact, various subjects have been discussed at length, some instigated by others. Many of these Geoff considered important enough to condense into information sheets which might be interesting to a wider audience. Some of the more generalised of these are included in this chapter. Geoff stresses always, these are his views gained from his own observations, perspective; and conclusions formed from his talks and studies since being in that dimension.

These appear in chronological order and some are dated. Where necessary, a brief explanation as to the inspiration provoking them, is included in brackets at the start.

(This was the first information we received and came about following queries about 'light workers' and their roles.)

# 1

A vast number of us reincarnated between 1934 - 1956 approximately. Although some arrived before, and many more have arrived since, and will still do so, those reincarnating during that time period were the vanguard who will begin the process and herald the changes, once activated.

Although the numbers are great, the groups are kept to small numbers who share common interests and ideals. This is to avoid personality clashes born out of years of negativity and confusion, and the possible disharmony this could cause.

During our childhood years, we were taught and advised by beings not on the planet. This was done while we slept and no doubt, parents etc., found we asked some daunting questions! But as we grew, peer pressure forced us to block out a lot of this knowledge although we all retain it within and can access it at any time. The one abiding factor none of us lost, was a deep sense of purpose and reason for being here.

Once we no longer accepted teachings from these outer beings we became vulnerable to opposing factions whose purpose was not in our, or the planets, best interests. We gave away much of our control and reality during this time and the 'purpose' became subdued and lost amidst all the confusion. However, each group had a leader', one who could pull it all together and regain balance. All of us have been joining up with other group members during sleep state for many years without realising this was going on apart from some residual 'leaking' through of information when this was necessary. These 'meetings' kept us supported and allowed vital information and guidance to be given, also, it 'inspired' us to obtain and read relative literature, and to form links at a physical level with each other as we recognised another group member, or one on the same mission. Although small, each group interacts with all the other groups to form a massive network across the entire planet.

Now time is crucial and the changes needed are being speeded up in all of us. It is important to remember that there are these opposing factors all around us who will try to reaffirm the negatives in everything. When you come across people you simply cannot 'gel' with, or those so out of sync. with yourself, they probably represent those factors. Unfortunately many in

120

positions of authority follow that pathway too. However, if you can flood them with light mentally, they should not be able to influence you again and you have much support all around you.

For now this is all you need to know. Just be willing to accept the changes going on within you and know you are being watched over. Be ready and willing to make a commitment to fulfil the purpose you are here for.

All forms of creation link those on this pathway. This includes art, music, inspired architecture; also those involved with healing in various forms including those in conservation projects, and of course, gardening and caring for animals. All of us are attracted to these pursuits in varying degrees because they are all linked to the overall purpose.

The long period of doubt and confusion is now almost at an end. It has been a difficult time but has not been without its reasons. Never forget you have full control of your life and your reality, now you know this and believe it, you will no longer be subject to the will or whims of anyone else. Never allow the doubts of others to influence your 'knowing' and your beliefs. There is nothing that cannot be possible.

October 1996

# 11

## Aspects Of Reality

Don't forget that what happens to us today, is tomorrow's memories. Once an event has happened, has passed, whatever it is, it only then exists in our memory. We can replay the event in our minds, and experience all the same feelings, emotions, etc., but it is still something that happened yesterday. We can never have exactly that same experience again. Similar yes, until we learn what they tell us, but never exactly the same.

We can file the experience in our subconscious store but unless it is observed and then filed correctly - i.e. in the correct category, namely a valued or otherwise experience, and let go of as such, it can leak out and affect our present.

Valued ones can be reviewed from time to time to give us upliftment and guidance, but those less than ideal, or even harmful, should be firmly locked away without judgement to prevent their influences causing effects now. Those can be reviewed better when we are no longer in physical life.

So what is our personal reality? A series of memories, or creating new ones? Our physical lives are a culmination of a series of memories to date. But it is the present that holds all power. Power that can be dissipated in reliving the past and wishing some things had been done differently. Simply accept you did the best you could at the time in the ever changing flow of life. If we view our memories objectively, our power can be reorganised and focussed to create with real intention, a future that leaves a wealth of remarkable experiences and memories. We create our experiences all the time, so we may as well decide to have only the ones we really want, choosing to focus on those rather than leaving it to random subconscious selection.

24th November 1996

# 111

(Following a letter extract and conflicting messages concerning the emotions, I asked Geoff the following questions:)

1. Some authors are saying that because of the light etc. that is being sent to Earth, the need for drastic change is no longer necessary and the majority of humanity will make it. That makes it sound as if not much is going to change at all, and things will jog along just the same as they have for years? However, looking around at people, they still seem to be lacking in consciousness and compassion, are still negative and mostly unchanged. They are still doing all the things harmful to the planet. Also, if so much is being done from off the planet, surely whatever role we might once have been required for, is no longer necessary and could be done just as easily from the Spirit Realms?

2. There also seems to be some confusion about our emotions. Should we be aiming for becoming totally devoid of personal emotions and and emotional love, and instead be operating only from universal, unconditional love?

Below are the comments Geoff made on these:

1. "Human nature is such that those still on the Earth and in tune, find it very hard to be specific about the exact extent of the changes. Few doubt change is vital, but while information is available, it is not easy for those incarnate to accept it unconditionally because of personal beliefs and limitations. Only those already off the planet have the courage to spell out the possibilities, knowing those here will find some of them extremely uncomfortable. They are only possibilities as events are evolving all the time, nothing is set in concrete, yet. But whatever does eventually occur, those who are working by using light at this time, have nothing to fear. Only those who cannot shift their belief and reality structures, fears, negativity etc., will experience more uncomfortable happenings.

It is probable a good ratio of humanity will make it but even so, this planet requires the removal of large sections because it is simply over-populated. To some extent this is being addressed naturally and population levels are dropping but not fast enough. The drain on natural resources is still taking too much from the planet and isn't being replaced and healed sufficiently to sustain the entire population. However uncomfortable it may be, many will have to be removed, maybe to an alternative Earth, maybe by electing to 'die' and mostly, they will be those who refuse to alter the habits and beliefs they have always held, and claim not to see any reason for change.

The role of those at the forefront is largely undefined. But it is still necessary. The energies required must be filtered/channelled through those here, it cannot be done adequately from off the planet, so this role is important."

2. "The emotions requiring release are those which hold us in states of negativity. It is those states that have created much of the problems in humanity to date. They have now served their purpose. However, while Universal love is desirable and necessary, we are not meant to operate on that alone. Universal love can take the place of negative emotions but we must have a balance and still need emotional love. It is very important for our well being and to prevent us becoming too detached. For an example; look at the present popularity of choosing to be single parent families. This is totally the wrong to go. It is vital for children to be brought up in a balanced environment if they are to achieve a healthy, happy life when adult. What example do they get with only one parent. This trend will reverse eventually as men become more balanced within themselves and therefore provide the qualities needed in an ideal partnership. Men and women must compliment each other totally, no power struggles or strategy games. Instead there must be trust, harmony and genuine love. If there are children, they should be conceived and raised in that vibration of love. And there must only be children who can be supported completely by their parents and by the planet. The idea that the purpose of a committed

partnership is only about producing children must go too. That is old thinking based on biased religious teachings and has no value at all in the future of the planet.

The important thing to remember is that for emotional love to work and give out the correct energies required by the planet, you must have the right partner. One at the same level as yourself who has gone through many lifetimes and experiences, some of these together, and who is balanced within. Anything less than that will be harmful and hamper your own abilities and progress. This cannot be stressed enough because many of the present negative vibrations on the planet have been caused by allowing a suffocating of our emotions to occur by remaining with the wrong partner, or by having far too many intimate partners. All those achieve is a complete blocking of your energy centres, and of all psychic abilities. The future of Earth requires harmonic co-operation throughout and this means the energies given out by Earth's occupants must have a firm basis in a definitive vibration of love and balance. This cannot be achieved if there is any element of discord."

22nd February 1997

# IV

## Genetically Engineered/Modified Foods

This is something I am totally opposed to. Any interference in the process of nature and natural growth will lead to problems that can not even be envisaged yet. It is as foolish as feeding meat products to herbivores and look where that has led!

The problem lies in finding ways of feeding more people than the planet can sustain. Failed harvests and changing weather patterns exacerbate the situation and it will reach crisis point. But genetic alterations are basically producing mutations in an attempt to ensure sufficient food. And if you feed people on mutations then it follows that mutated people will result. The horrific consequences of this will be appalling because for all their qualifications, these scientists do not really know what they are doing in the long term. They can only hazard guesses and hope, not an ideal to live by and really, the public is being used in a huge and extremely dangerous experiment because research can only truly be done out in the field. By the time results filter through, it will be too late for many things.

This Earth will need to go back to more natural ways of producing foods. No more use of chemicals and harmful substances, but respect and healing for the soil, and the positive influence of unpolluted organic materials to enrich naturally. Then what is grown will be truly nourishing in every way, including Spiritually because when things are grown naturally in this way, they are infused with Spiritual energies too. Modified foods will be dead energies that lower nutritional balances. Foods must be eaten as fresh as possible to sustain not only the body, but all the levels within the body including the soul.

There will be much greater and profound connections and communications between the physical and the Spiritual worlds, also between other worlds. This will mean the availability of compatible foods from those worlds that cannot even be imagined yet.

Late November 1997

# Addendum

This whole subject is being carefully monitored in these dimensions. It is causing a lot of concern because of the implications. You are being controlled by the power and money of the big corporations, businesses that have a vested interest in promoting these foods, businesses that produce chemical substances that harm the planet. There is a growing risk you will no longer have any choice in what you eat, and those who select organic foods as the healthier and preferable option, will find they can no longer be grown without cross-contamination from modified crops.

Quite apart from the horrific possible consequences of these poorly researched 'tainted' crops - mutations that may occur in other species because all will be susceptible to the pollen from these crops distributed on the wind, much wildlife will become extinct as habitats and feeding zones disappear; and there are greater risks not yet addressed.

You are left in ignorance about the exact levels these genetic experiments can attain in the minds of these seeking to control. Levels which will effect every life, and may well be used in selection processes about life itself. However much there will be arguments against, it will become possible for genes to be introduced into foods that can control behaviour, health, intelligence, and ultimately, life and death. You are being fooled into believing what is being done is a benefit. The only real benefit will be in the wallets of the company heads. It is ultimate control, the ultimate nightmare; and worse, one that even those producing these crops cannot estimate. It must be stopped at all costs. Every thinking person must make their own protest against this, and support every effort to prevent modified crops ever being planted.

It cannot be stressed enough what an opportunity this is for compassionate people to make themselves heard and respected. And it is a protest that must be won, for the sake of the future of the planet.

12th July 1998

# V

(I asked Geoff for his opinion on a life of service, also about putting the needs of others before our own selves if this proves detrimental.)
First and foremost, the only responsibility we have is to ourselves. We must not take on responsibility for anyone else, ever. In doing so, we actually take over control of part of that person's life and this is a definite no go area in incarnational terms.

If we assume responsibility for others in any way, we find limitations and restrictions affect our own lives. This is because in taking that control in other's lives, we are preventing them from gaining their own experiences, and we can even block them from the natural flow in their own lives. This is wrong and affects us as a way of showing us we are in error. It is also cause and effect, and can even result in poor health which diminishes our bodily energies. All of this is attracted as a way of saying 'let go' of hanging onto responsibility for others and look to yourself.

This is not being selfish. Our duty is to maintain ourselves first. How can we be useful in any way if we are below par?

I cannot fully agree with a life of service being the only reason being here. Experiencing is the reason for incarnating for the majority. Those who have become highly evolved through gaining all experiences, have a choice of living in the higher realms, or coming back to teach. The latter choice does mean a life of service with greater rewards upon returning home.

Certainly this would apply to those such as Sai Baba.

It is easy to become confused by such examples. But we all serve in some way and this does not have to mean self sacrifice. In fact, this is not recognised as valid. Those choosing to sacrifice themselves have to experience life and although the work they do is recognised, if worthwhile, shutting themselves off from life gains them no rewards.

There are many, many ways of serving. Respecting others and simply making sure you always give out what you would wish to receive back, is a perfectly valid way of service. Even 'being cruel to be kind', is regarded as service if done correctly. Artists serve by bringing pleasure to others, yet their life-styles could be seen as totally self indulgent to some.

It all boils down to interpretation and as we know, that can be a very personal thing depending on background, society, and at the risk of offending, religion. Your first 'duty' always, is to yourself. Do the best you can for yourself, but unselfishly if possible , and it follows you will do your best in your dealings with others. By unselfishly I mean be firm, but in consideration of other's feelings, not deliberately causing hurt. A refusal given in the right way won't cause resentment.

Anything that causes restrictions in your life, blocks you, or makes you ill, is wrong in some way, and must be released for the flow to resume. When it is right, everything goes right for you and the flow is evident.

8th April 1997

## VI

(This followed a query requesting further clarification on this subject, in personal terms.)

# Soul Groups

Sizes of soul groups vary from two or four, up to hundreds or more. The larger ones are usually further behind in evolutionary terms, and often divide into sort of sub-groups depending on what is required.

At the very beginning, the outward journey of soul groups before fragmentation, the purpose is a mission to go out and learn, experience, always in a vibration of love. If you think about how dropping a stone into water sends out ripples, this is something like the layers represented in soul groups. It is like a pyramid of groups, each spreading out below but all interconnected. What this means is that not everybody you deal with is part of your group. Even family members may come from a different group but can connect with yours to gain certain lessons or experiences which can then be taken back as examples to their particular group.

Not everyone in your circle of family and friends, will all be in the same group as you. Casual acquaintances may or may not be. However, there is usually a sense of affinity with members of your own group, and a feeling of 'knowing' although the strength of this knowing is dependent on how closely linked you are, in spiritual terms. There will always be more detachment with those from other groups, even if forming family member roles in that lifetime.

You do not always stay within the same group through each lifetime. As in any group, some wish to evolve quicker and therefore, may move upwards into another grouping, to enable them to do so. Sometimes we can also move down to act in a teaching capacity to help another group. This though, is more likely with those highly evolved. However, those who are closely bonded, always move on together so you are never alone, or without those you have known for thousands of years and through many lifetimes. And eventually, the entire original group will all join up again.

Apart from group members, we can gain lessons and experiences by arranging these in sleep state with any individual who can provide what is needed. This is always a mutual arrangement which benefits both. The connections don't ever really end. You always 'belong', in the sense that however highly evolved you become, you are still part of a group. No being was ever meant to be alone and even the Creator gains from experiencing our interactions. Nothing stays static and all is required to bring perpetual evolvement and progression.

Apart from our personal required experiences and lessons, groups are selected for certain tasks depending on their evolutionary gains. Training can be given to help us in this work, which we agree on before reincarnating. Even after reincarnating, training goes on during sleep state. However, we all have free choice and can choose to reject the work at any time. Often, not all the group come back at the same time, and some remain in spirit to give help and support from there. Sometimes this work is completed without any conscious awareness at all throughout life, only accessed and realised after passing into the spiritual dimensions.

In terms of evolutionary percentages, you may think of our group as being between 65% - 70%. There are no 'leaders' in groups, all are equal, however there are usually more evolved guides who can act as leaders to pull groups together. Where there is any mixing of groups, you will find yourself drawn to supporting and assisting those from your own group first and foremost. This always takes precedence.

Late April 1997

# VII

(This subject came up as a query in a group sitting. Discussing it afterwards, Geoff decided it may be helpful to pass on details of an exercise he discovered. Although suitable for all, this was actually given for women uncertain how to empower themselves.)

## On Poweʀ Anò Sensualíty

You may find some of this uncomfortable. If so, I make no apologies but would suggest it is an area within you that needs attention because it has been neglected. It has to do with accepting yourselves and embracing every aspect of that. Only by doing so, can you be whole and fully empowered.

To start with, the very best way of exploring your sensuality in through intimate contact with another person. But it is essential it is the 'right' person, someone you have known, evolved and developed with, and loved for many thousands of years. Someone you trust completely, who is balanced and therefore not in need of any psychological games of control as ego boosts.

At this time, most of you are not in that ideal relationship but with partners for other mutual reasons of growth, some of these reaching cyclical conclusion to free you for new pathways. Others have someone currently 'invisible' in other worlds. You can be aware though that does not necessarily rule out such contact. In fact, much more than you realise can occur during your sleep state, with your subconscious permission; but through your thinking based on conditioning of control and limitation, it is veiled and confined to your subconscious on return to your physical body.

However, for the purpose of this exercise, I will keep it to developing your own power and balance within. Firstly, throw out all ideas of anything being wrong about sensuality. You have been fed a diet of myth towards this by those who were fearful of the power women are capable of when fully acknowledging this area. Secondly, separate it totally from

132

sexuality. Linking the two is a whole different subject and it is important to balance and empower yourself before tackling it.

Most people have something they like to touch which gives them pleasure. For example, various materials such as velvet, marble, a leaf or flower petal, animal's fur, even your own skin, and so on. Often you have no idea why you experience pleasure like that and it stops at a outer level. What happens is a mutual exchange of energy. Every single thing has energy. When you touch something, that energy is exchanged to mutual benefit and pleasure. That is sensuality in a nutshell.

Most leave it at that but the knack comes in developing it further by experiencing it at chakra level. At this stage, you will realise the role and importance of the chakras. That usually surfaces early in any Spiritual teachings. Start with the two lower chakras. These are about you, your personality and experiences. The very essence of your being at this stage in your evolvement. When you feel that pleasure in touching something, try to experience it in the lower chakra. Transfer the feeling of pleasure from your hand and sense it as pleasure in that area. This is actually quite simple and not as difficult as it may sound. All such sensations are registered in your brain which conducts along neurons, so with practice, linking by thought the sense of touch with your lowest chakra area, you will feel a sensation rather like a warm pleasant flush infusing that area. That is the energy stimulating the chakra which will spin. It is surprising how much energy can be exchanged and generated in this way. Once you have achieved that and know the feeling you are aiming for, you can lift it to the next chakra, experiencing it in both. Don't rush it! It can be a very powerful sensation. Take your time, you have been subdued in this area for a very long period of lifetimes, so don't expect instant miracles. Continue working on it until eventually you can lift it right up through the chakras which will all spin in unison creating a complete balancing throughout the body. This in turn sends energy to all the cells creating health throughout. You will feel good all over. It creates a tremendous sense of well being and inspires good health. You will feel powerful and know your power is returning intact because this energy will also connect you to your Spiritual self and works through all levels bringing greater awareness.

Depending on how well you do, you may find you experience a tingling all over, and sometimes, a slight shaking as you reach the top two chakras. Don't be concerned by this, it is perfectly natural and passes once all the energy is utilised.

Once your chakras, body and cells have absorbed all the energy they can take, the residue can be released through the crown chakra. This infuses your aura and then goes out into your surroundings affecting not only other people, but also the planet which takes up that energy with amazing keenness. Remember though, the only valid and positive energy is one created in a love vibration because that is what is so desperately needed for Earth now, and why, when you are relating to another person, it must be the right vibration. When you become really proficient, you can experience wave after wave of this energy rising through the chakras which is not only vitalising, pleasurable and empowering to you, but pours out vast amounts of energy to heal, help and uplift the planet and all around you. You can understand from this why it has suited the negative forces to keep this subject so suppressed and hidden until now.

The beauty of this method is you can see quick results. There is no need to drag up old emotions and clear blockages first because the chakras will do all that once fully operational.

One minor warning, when you become whole and empowered in this way, you will give out a vibration of sensuality. Light and love will protect you but you may find it sometimes attracts men unbalanced on the masculine side and thus confused. These men are drawn to sensuality like a moth to a flame, but you will be very aware they are not 'right' for you and can repel them. Just be aware it can happen.

May 1997

# VIII

## Anger

## Our Motivation To Seek Within

There cannot be many experiencing life on Earth, who haven't felt anger in some degree. Mild irritation aside, it is the excess of anger which tells us a lot about ourselves and where we are at. Make no mistake, anger is a destructive force and always turned inwards.

We have many clues in our lives as to the lessons and learning we need for our progression, and it is progression at the heart of incarnation. Through progression our souls evolve as we learn, experience, and work out cause and effect in our dealings with others.

So where does anger fit in, how does it help us? Anger is just such a clue. When we feel anger boiling up to the point we feel almost explosive, where we lose the ability to acknowledge another viewpoint or opinion, be very sure you are masking an area in yourself that needs attention. An area deep within that remains unrecognised and therefore, unhealed. You may feel your anger is directed at something or someone else, but that is only the catalyst, the mirror reflecting back at you your own inner discomfort. It is your own attraction of need, creating the circumstances to show you what you need to find, that inner conflict that puts you out of balance.

Anger can show us many things. Take a really extreme example of anger - that of 'road rage' or any other 'rage'. This is anger that can, and has, spilled over into violence and even killing. Although relevant, there is no point in going into the arrangement made between the parties involved because that is another subject. The point of such rage is it shows the person 'raging' they are out of control and in need of self-examination to discover why. A very necessary lesson emerging at just the right time.

There is another aspect of anger which can be picked up and used by negative forces for their own ends. That is where anger is a cover for our unacknowledged fears. These fears hold us back and block, until they are surfaced, faced and released, thus preventing negative forces from further hold on us.

But in all these cases, the anger, whatever form it takes, is not directed outwards however much we may argue otherwise, it is always aimed at ourselves with the purpose of saying this inner conflict is ready to be resolved. Anger is negative. It can not solve anything on its own merit. In fact, in any argument, the moment someone gets angry, they have lost the argument because reasonable debate is no longer possible.

Part of growing up is learning to deal with anger. Young children are often angry in their haste to achieve, and frustrated when unable to do something before they are ready, or to have things all their own way. They lash out and throw tantrums, not acceptable behaviour, so they are encouraged to channel that anger into positive pursuits by enlightened parents. It is no different once we are 'adult'. We can turn our anger into positive pursuits, in this case, by finding and healing that inner conflict.

It is not difficult to see from this, that anger is actually a spontaneous primitive/childlike reaction. We lose our objectivity once anger is aroused, and from then on, we shut off our learned civilised abilities such as listening to and respecting others, even if we are not in agreement. The ego takes over and promotes our desire to shout down what we then perceive as the opposition because we don't like what our anger is really showing us.

The very first thing to do when you find yourself getting angry, once that anger abates a little, is ask yourself why whatever it was, made you react in that way. But do be completely honest. It is no good trying to fool yourself, you have been doing that too long, hence the anger. Ask questions, let the answers surface honestly, and you will find the cause within.

Be wary of thoughts like 'there is nothing wrong with me, I don't need this', because you can be sure you do. Anger tells you so. When you have progressed enough, there is no need for anger because awareness and understanding take precedence. Part of progression means acknowledging other views and opinions without feeling personally threatened because you know you are balanced within.

It may be of interest that even here, we still make mistakes at times. We have a long way to go before reaching any 'perfection'. But there are always guides to help us learn from these. However, these guides, who are from higher levels and therefore, more evolved, never, never, react with anger, however provoked. Why? Because they have been there, worked through it all both on Earth and afterwards, in the etheric realms, and gained all that was needed for progression to true understanding. That is why they are so capable and willing to help us, and we in turn use our knowledge to help those on lower levels. So it was always intended to be on Earth because life on Earth really isn't all that different to life here. Perhaps with enough knowledge channelled through, and stereotyped beliefs rejected, that aim can finally be achieved.

July 1997

## IX

(This is an answer to a specific question directed to Geoff. The question was about how what we think and believe affects the kind of afterlife we create for ourselves?)

This is a very interesting question and one that actually covers a very broad spectrum, which is why it required careful thought before answering. The answer not only applies to the etheric realms, but also has relevance for the physical world too.

First, try to form a picture of these worlds and how they relate to each other. The place where we go after 'death' isn't somewhere 'way up there' as is often described in religious and general terms. There are distortions, but the worlds do interpenetrate, particularly on the lower scale of the etheric, and the astral worlds which are denser than the etheric but not quite so dense as Earth. The physical level is always the densest but all levels depend on all others within creation. It is possible therefore, that within any given area on Earth, there is also one more of the astral and etheric areas too. Just because they are 'invisible' doesn't mean they don't exist and in the same place.

This forms the basis of what you are questioning. Each time you think something, good or bad, that thought creates somewhere. What you perceive as reality around you, has been formed by your beliefs and thoughts over the years of your present incarnation, and in some cases, with residues from previous ones. Unless someone has exactly the matching beliefs, programming and thoughts as yourself, what they see around you will not be the same as your perception.

Many of the thoughts you have - and our thoughts do create every single moment - will not match your present idea of 'reality'. You may wish for something that inwardly, you feel is impossible for you at the present time. That does not invalidate your thought. It merely 'stores' it elsewhere, usually in the etheric realms. It waits there until one day you might release your inner block and create it in your lifetime, or until you go home and achieve greater awareness to accept it then.

It is the denseness and other factors, that make the physical the hardest realm to create in. And the hardest to discreate realities you no longer want. But, and this is part of the answer, whatever is created, never ceases to be. Therefore, whatever is perceived in the etheric realms, exists. Alien realms exist. They are and always will be. Many people do not believe there is life on other worlds so they are veiled from seeing those realms when in the etheric. Those same people might have another incarnation where something triggers more open mindedness and then, when back in the etheric, they can visit those realms. They, like the other realms certainly exist. They have been formed and worked on over countless aeons of time. They constantly evolve through the thoughts that create within them. The basics are always there since their original creation. Just as the basics of the physical world is always there, but it is the thoughts of those on Earth that create all the different realities.

Equally, the thoughts of those on Earth can affect the etheric realms at lower levels. But here, thoughts create much faster, for example, to travel somewhere it is enough to simply think of the place you want be, to be there in an instant. If a longer route is desired, that is possible too. Free will is still paramount, and some enjoy walking. Here, there is more understanding of how thought creates though, and therefore more responsibility attached to it.

What it boils down to is consideration of what is actually 'real'. You will think the home you live in is real because it is there and you see it. But all it is really are atoms held together through thoughts, thoughts you, and others, are not even aware of thinking. Your home was created and then built in a process involving designers, architects, builders and so on. It is possible, the end result was quite different in many respects, to what was in the thoughts of the original designer. This is because at each stage, other thoughts came into play. Your home is reality to neighbours, but they will not actually see it in exactly the same way you do. All these people involved in some way concerning your home, gives an example of group creation, something that also explains how things 'exist' around us even if not our actual creation through thought.

To give a more personal example, your physical body is equally held together by your thoughts. You create it moment by moment, but, after you no longer need it, when you return to the etheric, it doesn't just cease to be. It transmutes to another form and even if cremated, the resulting ash never ceases to be. The you created in that lifetime, always leaves a tiny particle behind. It is the same here, something always remains of what has been created. Like most of us, you may have certain beliefs of what to expect after death. Whatever they might be, that is the 'reality' you will find. Apart from extremes such as those who believe they will end up in hell, your corner of the etheric will create your belief. Eventually, if those beliefs are erroneous, you will seek guidance which is always available, and a truer reality emerges. But it is still your reality, yours alone, or shared and co-created with another in harmony. The life you then lead will be of your choosing. Would you have it any other way given free will?

To sum up then, and as you can now see, your question has far wider implications; in one sense, yes, what you think and believe creates your afterlife. But, you are not alone. You are part of a group, each of that group having their own thoughts and creating their own bit of it. You will interact with them and therefore you have the wider version. It is just like on Earth really.

Perhaps one last example to make it as clear as possible. There are people who believe in there being nothing after death. They have no perception of any realm or reality. Having 'died' and discovered they wander around utterly lost until rescued, those people still have no idea of anything by way of non-physical reality. Any thoughts they did give to it, would most likely centre on it as a black void of total unconsciousness, and since the consciousness never dies, nor does the spirit/etheric body, they cling to the only 'reality' they can imagine, Earth, totally bewildered. However, once rescued they are taken to the realms of light and find, usually to their amazement, here is a place rather like Earth with people, buildings, landscapes, etc. So although those people believed in nothing coming afterwards, and in a sense experienced that for a while, eventually they found to their joy, a whole world and a life to be part of. A world that exists because of the thoughts of many who have gone before and have now evolved further. Gradually the non-believers will learn how to create the things that matter to them, find group companions and experience their creations too.

The etheric and physical worlds did not always exist. They were formed and created millions of years ago by early pioneers on this journey we all undergo. Those pioneers, sent and assisted by the Creator, formed these worlds from their own thoughts and ideas. Basically, they still exist as such, but have changed and evolved just as the Earth has, built on and added to by the countless thoughts and visions of others, creating, recreating and co-creating, again and again, through

**141**

evolution and progression as we all move higher and higher in our spiritual development. Nothing stands still unchanged forever, wouldn't it all become very boring and tedious if it did?

I hope you feel this has answered your question adequately. It wasn't an easy one because there is no cut and dried, simple explanation. That is one reason why there are so many different theories about life beyond the physical realm. That makes it very confusing for those seeking the truth of it all, and why none of us has any right to say our findings are absolutely the way it is. It is our way which we present as our theory. One of many theories which fall like raindrops, and like raindrops, each can be taken up or not, refreshing and nourishing when and where needed.

10th. August 1997


# X

## Reincarnation

Reincarnation is not an automatic right. It depends on how the last lifetime progressed. Where further lessons and experiences are required, and can only be learned through physical incarnation, then it is a case of waiting for the correct circumstances and conditions to arise. We do not reincarnate ad lib. Certain challenges are necessary to present us with exactly what we seek. Sometimes these conditions may not arise for many earth years. At our level, it is rare to reincarnate very quickly. Even when conditions do arise, we still have free will and that is paramount. The incarnation must be wanted totally, without exceptions. The choice is always ours and while there are close bonded links still fulfilling the present incarnation most prefer to wait until those links also pass over.

It is a little different at earlier levels. There, where much learning etc., is still required, incarnations tend to occur more frequently, and preference is always given to those requiring the most learning/lessons/experiences still. Also at those levels, we are not yet at the stage of fully recognising close bonds with group members. It is a bit like nursery school to give a simile. We have friends etc., at nursery school but rarely do these remain so throughout life. As we grow/ progress, we form more lasting relationships although often, even these suit a purpose and move on. But some remain throughout life, such as parents, siblings, offspring etc. Once we pass over, we recognise those links and the roles they undertook in our lives, and we have no wish to reincarnate on until we can be reunited with those particular group members at their passing. Sometimes we like to help them in ways we are permitted; sometimes we want to be in contact where awareness allows this. Where there is an even stronger bond, and particularly, the strongest of all, it is common to wait for that one to join us, even more so if the last lifetime was spent apart in any way.

As we evolve, it is usual for soul group members to reunite and share experiences, learning etc. This is because we do not all have every single possible experience going. Here we can learn in that way and gain in our own progression. If necessary, it is even possible through a process something like a semi-merging, sleep/dream state, to actually have certain required experiences yourself, without the need to incarnate for them. This is more common towards the end of the incarnational round.

Occasionally, even at earlier levels, there can be a long wait to reincarnate. If the passing followed a lengthy and harrowing illness, it might mean a long period of rest and recuperation before another life can be undertaken. Also, those whose belief structures result in them being unable to accept their deaths, those who need rescuing and taking to the light, can take a very long time to gain that acceptance. If they are unable to accept they have actually survived 'death', when their belief was in nothing afterwards, then accepting they can have a life over here, followed by another on Earth in due course, is mind blowing.

There are always exceptions of course, and nothing is cast in concrete. Sometimes paradoxically, even at higher levels there are those who reincarnate quickly. These are usually those who accept a sudden and early death, for example, the murder of a child, an unexpected abortion, or something similar which terminates an otherwise normal incarnation. These are not 'victims' because there are no victims, and even babies create and accept their realities.The reincarnating spirit has after all, selected that parentage and conditions for what it needs to learn and experience. But sometimes a certain unplanned experience is required and mutually accepted, and where possible, an earlier reincarnation arranged as a result. This can also happen where a seemingly ideal incarnation goes wrong. Although rare, this can occur and it is better to leave it and start again, rather than it be wasted. Our physical lives are not pre - set, and open out in an ongoing process as we create and attract what we need, therefore circumstances that appeared ideal to start with, may alter, and cannot always fit in with what is required by the soul at that time. This can be, although not in every case, the explanation behind the death of a young person with seemingly, everything to live for. Some take comfort in saying how unfair this is, but really, it is perfectly worked out for the benefit of all concerned. Only physical limitation views it otherwise.

So, to sum up, reincarnation is subject to numerous conditions and dependant on a huge variety of needs and circumstances, but always, free will is paramount and cannot be overlooked. In general terms, the more evolvement/progress needed, the quicker you reincarnate. The closer you get to the end of the physical incarnations, you less ardently you seek them. That doesn't necessarily mean you are then highly evolved, far from it, it just means you have gained enough to continue progressing in spirit without the need to take on physical life again, unless choosing to do so in a teaching capacity. This is sometimes offered as a way of giving service, to balance wrongs, and to advance progression to a higher level.

24th August 1997

# XI

(This subject was discussed quite early on in our contact and has recently been updated as Geoff learned more. He stresses there is no intention on his part of being judgmental, but he truly believes now, through understanding this, and how it relates to why we are here, and what life is all about, it will help many to create much better lives all round. And that is something that will not only benefit humans, but all things on our world.)

## Personal Responsibility

This subject is of vital importance to each and every human, and understanding it cannot begin too early in life. Unless you can take in and fully comprehend this concept, you will remain stuck in a state of victim mentality and blame. The trend for far too long now, has leaned towards a wimpish society unable to accept the role of creating their own lives in every way. Encouragement from those with a vested interest in ruling lives, has led to beliefs in total helplessness and ineffectiveness. This results in a need to blame anything and anybody else for everything that happens. Ultimately, the endgame will produce a nation of malleable people totally out of self control, who will seek redress for the slightest thing, need help and counselling to cope with everyday events, and scared of their own shadows.

Part of the problem is an enduring belief in fate. The notion that major events in our lives are out of our hands, inevitable, because fate deems it so. Or, that it is God's Will and as such, unavoidable. Blaming God for some of the ghastly events that happen, credits this supreme force with a total lack of compassion, and gives no understanding to the 'gift' of individual free will. It would do well to remember, those who preach of things being God's Will are themselves human beings with all the human failings of limitation and misinterpretation!

Why do reasonably intelligent beings seem happy to believe their lives are not under their own control? Does that really make it easier to accept the 'horrors' of life that can occur? I don't think so. In fact, I think it makes the impact of those events far harder and the resulting need to blame, traps people in a rut that can influence and overshadow the rest of their lives.

I have no wish of minimising the impact of such things as violent crime, or anything else that seriously disrupts normal life. But, I do want to demonstrate how a different approach and greater understanding can help to overcome submergence into a victim mentality that can ruin your entire life.

Personal responsibility is a Spiritual principle. However much you may wish to get away from it in physical life, you cannot escape the consequences over here because often, ignoring this or refusing to accept it results in further karma (cause and effect).

Let me try and put this across in the simplest terms, whatever happens to you throughout your life, your physical incarnation, is a product of your own creation brought about through many reasons. Reasons that could go back to something uncompleted from another lifetime, or, part of the learning or karmic balancing you have agreed to for this one. Even being born with some disfigurement or disability comes under this umbrella. The difficulty most have with understanding this, is in seeing this present lifetime as the only one you will have. It is distressing to see small children with enormous problems, but becomes far more enlightening when you can gain awareness of the fact that children born now, ended another lifetime as adults who perhaps left learning or balancing unresolved. And don't such things teach us all compassion?

The other problem with acceptance of this principle, apart from the necessary amnesia, is in placing physical life as all important. It is of course, important, but your real life and home is in Spirit, All physical things pass away, physical life is transient and nothing of physical life lasts. These facts cannot be denied. You come into physical life with a new personality and nothing else, except an inner blueprint of things to be achieved in that life. At the end of it, you go home taking nothing with you apart from those achievements which will be assessed, and your next physical life will be determined by that, as will your life in this etheric dimension,

All that forms part of your physical life, material things, and those who shared your life, cannot go with you. Once over here, you soon see things in their true reality, and since you can never have that physical lifetime again, it has gone forever, hankering after anything that was part of it, is totally pointless, as you quickly realise.

One of the ways understanding about personal responsibility can help you, is by letting go. Most humans have great difficulty with this. They allow events and relationships that are long since over, to keep on affecting them, instead of detaching and moving on. Realising those events etc., were for a purpose, even if that purpose isn't obvious, does make it easier to put it all behind you and get on with your life. That doesn't meaning forgetting, but it is a fading of things so they cannot keep influencing your new choices. Harbouring bitterness and resentment over something won't change a thing, but it can and will harm you, eventually causing possible health problems as an outward manifestation of the inner turmoil.

Most people experience a broken relationship in various ways during their lifetime. Many will blame that on some cause or another, and spend varying amounts of their lives in trying to hang onto something that has served its purpose and will not come around again. Accepting personal responsibility means looking at the whole thing from another angle, questioning what you learned from it, perhaps accepting it was a karmic balancing even if the reason is unknown, and moving on from that experience renewed, to embrace the next part of your life. It may still hurt, but even hurt is something we choose to experience. Believing that others deliberately hurt us is an ego thing and as such, is really quite selfish. It doesn't allow for the feelings of the other person, and their need to live their own life. Personal responsibility also realises we are each individual and we cannot live our lives through anyone else, or rely on anyone else to make us happy.

Even excessive grief is also largely selfish. Grief at the loss of someone you cared for, is a necessary detachment and healing process. It takes time to adjust to life without someone who may have shared a significant part of that life with you. But letting go and moving on is something we all have to learn, it is essential for our own well-being. Refusing to let that person go by prolonged grieving is pointless because it isn't going to alter anything, except to harmfully affect you and deny you the further rich experiences of life. Selfishness comes into it when speaking only of personal loss without considering the happiness and freedom from restrictive conditions of the other person. Personal responsibility teaches us we need to become complete within ourselves, not reliant on any other.

Those who experience various crimes, also often hang on to the effects of that, blaming the perpetrators for restrictions to their lives. Sometimes if severe enough, it can cause the sufferer to allow the experience to ruin the remainder of that life, never moving beyond it. But in doing so, they allow just that one moment to go on controlling them. They give away power to the perpetrators constantly, replaying the incident again and again, focussing on that to the exclusion of all else. In doing so, they attract other negative events because of that focussing. Yet there are shining examples of those who have experienced and overcome all these things, some quite appalling, and have found those experiences the catalysts leading to a strong and rewarding life afterwards. In these, Divine purpose in action can be seen, and often, the forgiveness too which is so necessary.

To summarise on what is really a vast yet basic subject, personal responsibility, or self responsibility as it is sometimes called, is accepting totally that your life and all in it, is down to you; no-one and nothing else can do it for you. Who you are and whatever life holds for you is your choice, some of those choices made before you were born into this life. The most important detail to remember is that we are all participants in this game, this massive drama called physical life. There are no victims, no betrayals, no accidents, nothing we ourselves don't activate for the purpose of learning/ balancing etc. If we hang onto the pain and hurts, that is our choice, not something forced on us by someone else. Healing and moving on is our own responsibility, any blame for not doing so is ours and ours alone. Blaming any other participants in the drama will not affect them, they have played their part as required, and their life is theirs to live, not ours. Any residue we retain to keep on haunting us, will only affect us. We all have the built in ability to heal, it is our challenge to do so and we each have the capacity to overcome all things. Doing so makes us grow, evolve, and that is the reason for physical life and all our experiences in it.

Personal responsibility means looking at the wider aspects, seeing purpose in all that happens to you, and not viewing it just from the position of 'me'. Don't allow your ego to convince you these things are done to you, accept your role in them as a means of learning and experiencing. Knowing you have created and/or attracted all the happenings of your life, and have agreed to even the worst of them, frees you from the 'monsters' they appear to be. When you believe you have no control over your own life, you deny your own Divine spark and allow the 'monsters' to rule you. Some learning in physical life is tough, but by doing your best to overcome it, move beyond it, even laugh at it, it won't swamp you. Perhaps you won't know all the reasons until you leave the physical, but you will have gained in strength and made tremendous progress. More than that, life will be better, fun even, because you will no longer fear what 'it might throw at you'. Instead, you can focus on the life you want, doing your best in every way because to do anything less will only let you down, and understanding personal responsibility means that is something you cannot accept.

Each life unfolds just like a dramatic role which one day must end. Good or bad, nothing of physical life lasts forever. Knowing the reasons can enhance the experience.

Updated 1998

# Chapter Thirteen

# Geoff's Home And Gardens In Spirit

It has been perhaps my greatest privilege and joy to regularly visit Geoff's home in spirit, and even more, to bring back the memory of those visits to physical consciousness. My understanding is that we all go into the spirit realms from time to time during sleep state, but rarely do we remember these visits. Acute trauma in physical life does seem to have an effect on awakening psychic abilities, and on bringing through to waking consciousness such memories. Events that shake us to the core physically, also seem to loosen our hold on the density in this dimension as being the only reality.

The home Geoff has now, appears as solid as homes here, but it is more like a living entity itself. One which responds to its occupants and is capable of expanding or contracting according to need. Thus, if a party or gathering is arranged, however many are present, it is never crowded. Divine perfection in operation.

Homes in spirit are built/created by those who love that work. Perhaps physical circumstances meant they never found the opportunity for such creative work while incarnate, but at last their artistic skills in that direction can be realised. And the only 'planning permission' required is love - love of creation in that work, and that love permeates every part of the buildings.

Geoff's home is made of stone and wood. It isn't easy to find words to describe these materials in physical terms, so great is the vibrancy of them in colour and vitality. There is plenty of space and not a lot by way of furnishings. Geoff says he has little need of 'belongings', beyond those providing the basics. Some of this non-materialistic viewpoint seems to have rubbed off on me. I have noticed during the course of my contact with Geoff, I am gradually becoming ever more disenchanted with material 'things'.

The stonework of the house has a permanent golden glow to it, as if bathed in the beautiful rays of a setting sun. Inside, no matter which direction windows face, there is always light flowing in, never harsh, just a gentle softness that illuminates everything, giving an essence of life to the natural wood.

Outside, Geoff has designed the gardens so each can be accessed via archways in the hedging, or similar in walls, each is separated by walkways of fragrant grass, and leading to them all is a magnificent pergola walk covered in varieties of clematis and honeysuckle. The gardens range in themes, from a multi-colour, abundant cottage style, to those with a spiritual purpose - one in shades of pink; one in gold, purple and white; one in blues and silver - and a huge rectangular area devoted to four different water features, combining the beauty of planting with the gentle natural sounds of moving water.

Each garden has discreet seating allowing for privacy to enjoy contemplation while soaking up the atmosphere - the colours, scent, and natural sounds. There is a sense of peace and tranquillity which is almost tangible, yet also, such vibrant life everywhere. Next to a natural woodland is the wildlife pond, huge and surrounded by a mixed planting of rushes, grasses, and many of the other plants found naturally in such a setting.

It will probably surprise some that there should be both a vegetable and a fruit garden, but the enjoyment of growing doesn't have to stop at ornamental species. Also, fruit and vegetables still have a purpose along with the various nut trees which are abundant everywhere. Produce from all of these are very high in energy and provide for those who, on these levels, retain a need and desire to continue the pleasure of eating. On Earth, we need food to sustain our physical bodies and without food, we would starve. There is not the same requirement in spirit of course, because the etheric/spirit body is maintained by energy, therefore the requirement is for ways of restoring and providing energy when necessary, and not at set regular times as in physical life. Just as here, there is an enjoyment of socialising too, and providing refreshments for visitors. When we take in nourishment on Earth, energies from what we eat and drink helps to maintain our etheric/spirit bodies too, something maybe not clearly understood, although the energy aspect of foods is measurable. It is the unseen, indefinable aspect that causes denial in some, of the existence of these other bodies. And yet, energy itself, is invisible.

Beliefs, free will, Divine perfection means there is no reason why you cannot also have sheds, greenhouses, frames, in fact anything else that completes the enjoyment of your chosen work and life between lives. The only limits are due to those in your own thinking, restricting yourself to how you believe it must be, according to physical definitions.

Your reality in those dimensions is as real there, as our reality is to us. The difference is in the speed of creation through thought. On Earth, we labour long and hard to manifest our thoughts into creation. In spirit, thought creates immediately and if anything, wanting to do things by a longer process requires even greater focussed thought. This in itself is a learning experience which no doubt benefits us in our next lifetime.

The ability to create immediately through thought does not come automatically on passing over. Each time we go back home into spirit, we usually move up a level as we evolve and progress. The higher we go, the easier this instant creation ability works, and often, some practise is required to master this when newly arriving in spirit. There is always help available but even so, early results can he hilarious when the thoughts are lacking in vital details, as Geoff discovered with much amusement, entertaining me with tales of his own, and other's endeavours in this area. Luckily mistakes are easily rectified and practise does indeed, perfect the skill.

Those who believe life beyond consists of nothing but eternal rest are in for a bit of a shock. There is rest of course, taken when needed, but life in spirit at Geoff's level, is very much like life on earth without the negative aspects. Thus, there are periods of work as well as rest and recreation. The lack of a time structure as we know it, means greater freedom to pursue these activities as and when desired.

Since being in that dimension, Geoff has requested, and been asked, to take part in a number of work projects. One of these involved going into a lower vibration level to teach those interested and making choices for a future life, about proper natural care of the earth. When eventually those souls reincarnate, that knowledge will be retained subconsciously and will gradually surface in the course of those lives. This is just one example of how we select certain aspects of our future lives for whatever purpose is required. These souls, if they fulfil their choices without allowing the ego side of physical free will to interfere, will do much to help restore areas of our abused planet. I am sure further opportunities for such work will manifest and Geoff will accept them all, so great is the need on Earth; and those learning now, can in due course, also teach others. The hope eventually, is for a vast network of souls incarnate, respecting the planet and its resources, and taking proper care in the maintenance of it.

It is a wonderful bonus for me to be able to share in the knowledge of various work projects Geoff undertakes, to see how much enthusiasm and love goes into them, and even more than that, to have this amazing understanding of how it all operates. How the dimensions interpenetrate and co-exist, to be able to grasp a few of the secrets of creation itself and what it is all about, and to know absolutely that the end of physical life is not an ending at all, but a marvellous exciting continuance of something begun a very, very long time ago.

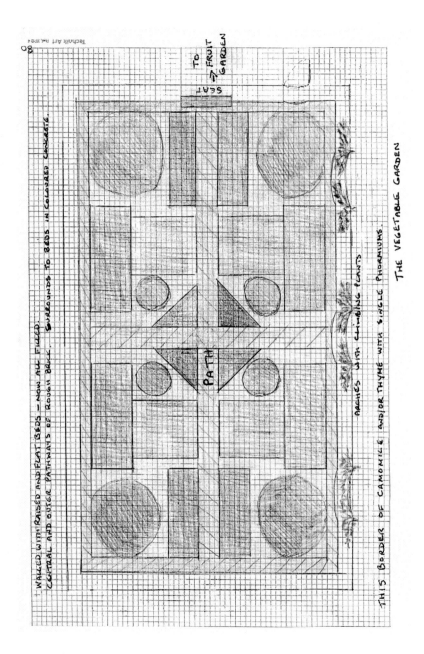

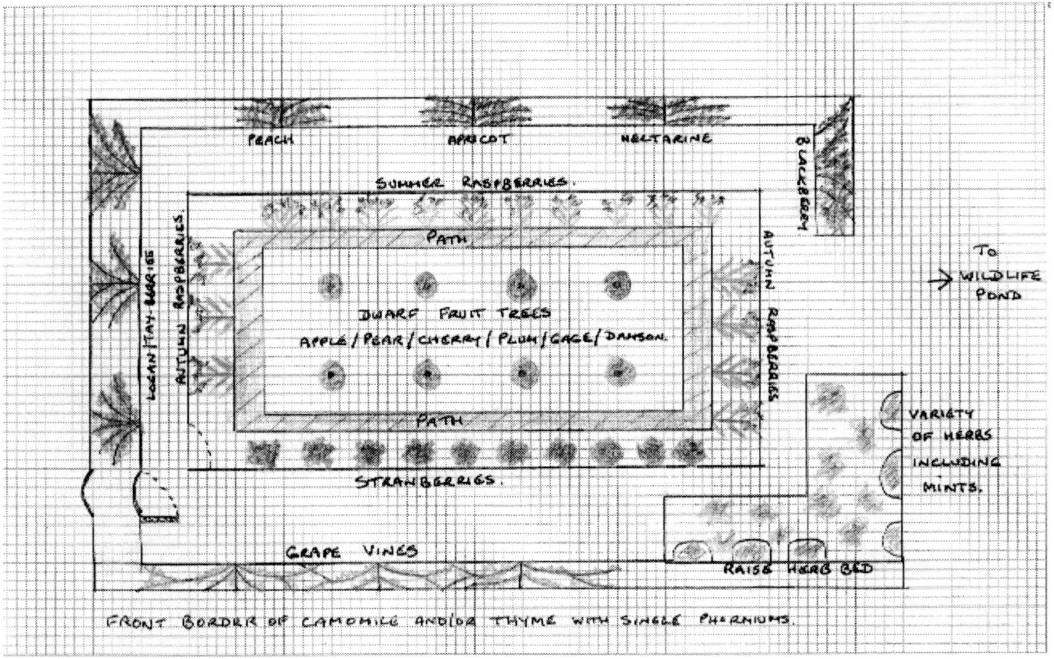

VARIETY OF HERBS INCLUDING MINTS.

BLACKBERRY

AUTUMN RASPBERRIES

RAISE HERB BED

NECTARINE

SUMMER RASPBERRIES

APRICOT

DWARF FRUIT TREES

APPLE/PEAR/CHERRY/PLUM/GAGE/DAMSON

PATH

PATH

PEACH

STRAWBERRIES

GRAPE VINES

AUTUMN RASPBERRIES

LOGAN/TAY-BERRIES

FRONT BORDER OF CAMOMILE AND/OR THYME WITH SINGLE PHARMIUMS

THE FRUIT GARDEN.

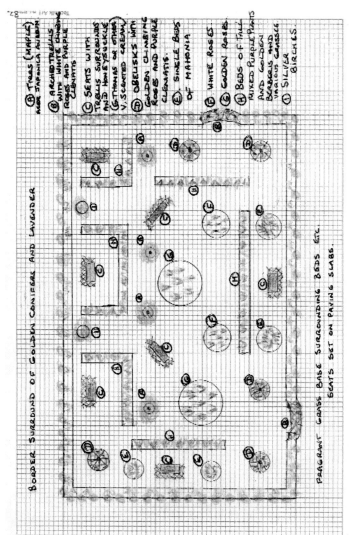

THE PSYCHIC GARDEN

A — TREES (MAPLES) ACER JAPONICA AUREUM
B — ARCHED TRELLIS WITH WHITE BUSH ROSES AND PURPLE CLEMATIS
C — SEATS WITH TRELLIS SURROUNDS AND HONEYSUCKLE (LONICERA OR OTHER V. SCENTED CREAM)
D — OBELISKS WITH GOLDEN CLIMBING ROSES AND PURPLE CLEMATIS.
E — SINGLE BEDS OF MAHONIA
F — WHITE ROSES.
G — GOLDEN ROSES.
H — BEDS OF TALL MIXED PURPLE PLANTS AND GOLDEN BERBERIS AND VARIOUS GRASSES
I — SILVER BIRCHES.

BORDER SURROUND OF GOLDEN CONIFERS AND LAVENDER

FRAGRANT GRASS BASE SURROUNDING BEDS ETC. SEATS SET ON PAVING SLABS.

YEW HEDGE.

(A) WEEPING WILLOW.

(B) SEAT WITH TRELLIS SURROUND COVERED WITH GOLDEN HONEYSUCKLE.

(C) ROSES.

(D) TRELLIS WITH PINK CLEMATIS. WHITE GERANIUMS AND SILVER VARIEGATED LONICERA.

(E) PURPLE BRONZE MAPLE, VARIETY OF HEATHERS PLANTS IN GOLD, WHITE, PINK AND MAUVE.

(F) TAMARISK, GOLD LONICERA, PURPLE HEUCHERA, SILVER VARIEGATED LONICERA.

(G) WEEPING CHERRY, LAVENDER.

(H) OBELISK COVERED IN WHITE CLIMBING ROSE AND PURPLE CLEMATIS UNDERPLANTED WITH LAVENDER.

(I) POND WITH PINK WATER LILIES WATER CASCADES OVER FLAT STONES FLANKED BY GRASSES ON ONE SIDE, PINK AND WHITE MARGINALS ON THE OTHER. PROBABLY OVER THE END.

'JEANNIE'S GARDEN'.

PLANTING ALL IN SHADES AND TONES OF PURPLE, PINK, GOLD, SILVER, WHITE AND CREAM.

**JAPANESE**
1. SEATS
2. SAND AND REEDS
3. PEBBLE WALKWAY
4. MOSS COVERED ROCKS
5. RED DWARF MAPLE
6. CLEAR POOL
7. PROSTRATE BLUE CONIFERS
8. GOLDEN ARGYRANTHEMUM
9. PINK PEONIES
10. PINK AND PURPLE CHRYSANTHS.
11. HEDGE OF ROSA RUGOSA

**MED IT (MEDITERRANEAN)**
1. SEATS
2. CARBONISED CONICAL CONIFERS
3. RECTANGULAR CHANNEL WITH RED WATER LILIES
4. FOUNTAIN HEAD
5. WHOLE LOT OF PLANTING IN HOT COLOURS
6. PAVING

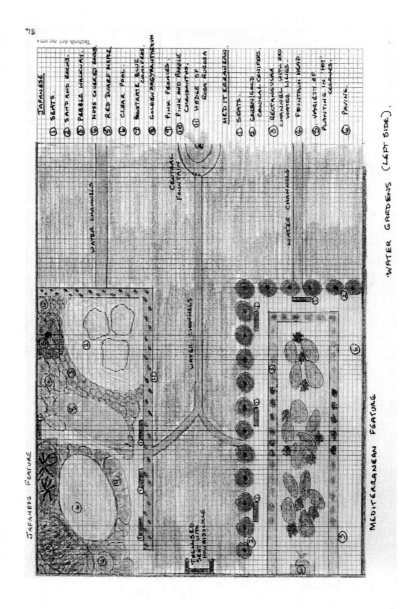

WATER CHANNELS

CENTRAL FOUNTAIN

JAPANESE FEATURE

MEDITERRANEAN FEATURE

WATER GARDENS (LEFT SIDE).

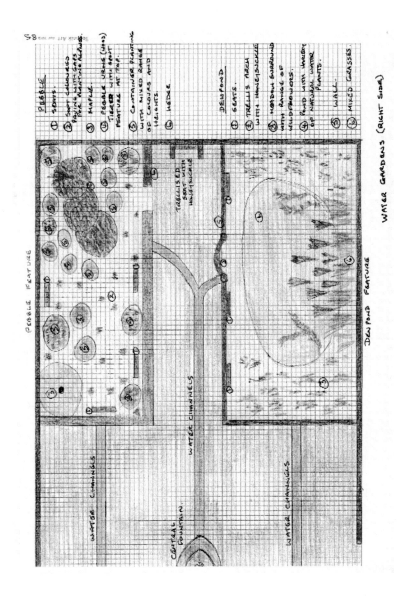

PEBBLE

SEATS.

① SOFT COLOURED
PAVING WITH GAPS
FOR PLANTING FEATURES.

② MAPLE.

③ PEBBLE URNS (HIGH)
TASTED WITH SPOT
FEATURE AT TOP.

④ CONTAINER PLANTING
WITH MIXED RANGE
OF COLOURS AND
HEIGHTS.

⑤ HEDGE

DEWPOND

① SEATS.

② TRELLIS ARCH
WITH HANDLES/CYCLING

③ MEADOW SURROUNDED
WITH RANGE OF
WILDFLOWERS.

④ POND WITH VARIETY
OF NATURAL WATER
PLANTS.

⑤ WALL.

⑥ MIXED GRASSES

PEBBLE FEATURE

DEWPOND FEATURE

WATER GARDENS (RIGHT SIDE)

TRELLISED
SEAT WITH
HONEYSUCKLE

WATER CHANNELS

WATER CHANNELS

CENTRAL
FOUNTAIN

WATER CHANNELS

WATER CHANNELS

161

# Chapter Fourteen

# Questions And Answers

Although Geoff has his own opinions on many subjects, and expresses them freely with little encouragement, there have been times when questions have arisen pertaining to other things. The interest we show is sufficient for Geoff to go and find answers for us wherever possible, and this chapter is devoted to some of the questions that have cropped up. Some of the information is from other sources via Geoff, and some from knowledge he has gained since passing over. As Geoff says, he has learned a lot already and is always eager to add to that because we are never beyond learning new things.

Q: Geoff, before we go on to general questions, can I ask, as I am sure many will, why did you decide to co-write this book?

A: Quite simply - need. The world is in a strange state at the moment and nobody knows which way things will go. There is little guidance, and what there is, is contradictory in many respects. I felt, having left the physical life fairly recently, it would be helpful to explain a few things as I see them from my perspective here. I am still 'in touch' with Earth, sufficiently to be able to relate to the kind of problems and concerns people may have. I am not saying my observations are wholly correct, but I am giving my thoughts from the level of understanding I have reached. People need hope, not the kind of scant information which can have us running around like headless chickens. I thought if I can explain what life is like on the other side of what is termed 'the veil', albeit at the

162

level I am at, it might give people something to cling on to. They have to know there is something more, something wonderful. A continuance of life without stress and hassles. They also need to understand why life on planet Earth must change, and I can give some words of wisdom on that too, which I have gained since being here.

Q: When you say your observations may not be wholly correct, what do you mean by that?

A: As I have tried to explain in my chapter on beliefs, there are many dimensions, many levels of understanding, and what you experience depends on what kind of belief system you have taken on board. That really is the crux of it all. What you believe to be true, is what you will find, but that can differ enormously according to your set, preconceived ideas. Those who's minds are more open, can access the true reality, the basic reality which is available for us all, and it is a pretty marvellous reality. What you believe colours that with the limitations and restrictions prevalent in most beliefs.

Q: I know you have covered this elsewhere, but it is such an important issue I feel some may like it explained here. Why is it that various accounts from those no longer in the physical, seem to differ in some important aspects?

A: I agree this is an important issue because it confuses those seeking to understand fully. It is all down to beliefs again and perhaps it would be helpful for me to give an analogy by way of example. Imagine for a moment you live on another planet and read books about life on Earth because you plan to visit one day. You have three books, one written by an African bushman, one by a Japanese, and one by a Westerner. Although many facts will agree, there will also be many that differ. For instance, each will say they go to bed at night and get up in the morning, have breakfast and go to work. But, the African will say he sleeps on the mud floor of his hut, has just leaves and nuts for breakfast, and works on the land. The Japanese will say he sleeps on a mattress on the floor with a wooden headrest, eats raw fish for breakfast before going off to work in the electronics factory. The Westerner says he sleeps in a soft bed with pillows and a duvet, has eggs, bacon, toast and coffee for breakfast before going by car to the office. Various other seemingly basic facts will differ too - clothing, religion if any, relationships - and if you read books by those from other countries, even other parts of countries, they would equally confuse. By now you are uncertain what to believe, which is correct? They all are of course, because so many factors relate to individual experience - culture, upbringing, beliefs, etc. But to someone never having been on Earth, it must seem that the differences mean one or more is inaccurate.

It is exactly the same here but if anything, there are far more levels and dimensions. Some are completely different, others vary in small ways; so you can see from that there will be differences in the accounts related because any of us can only describe things from our own level of understanding. It is the responsibility of the reader to accept what feels comfortable and gloss over what doesn't feel right for them. All accounts are sincerely given and nothing is ever forced on anyone. What you find unacceptable will not be your personal experience.

Q: Thank you for giving us such simple examples. While on this subject, is there any way you could help us to understand how the dimensions interrelate? We seem to have been given ideas that 'Heaven' is way 'up' there somewhere, but many from 'over' there say you are around us all the time?

A: This is another example of misleading information, mostly coming from religious sources unfortunately, and misinterpreted. All worlds are one. That is the first fact to grasp. It is because of the different vibrations that there can be many dimensions existing in the same space. The best analogy I can think of is a section of an ancient tree. This will have multiple rings radiating out from the centre. If you take the very centre one as being physical life, the densest level, then move outwards as through the astral realms and into the etheric dimensions, until you reach the outer ring which represents the finest vibration. Yet all are there in that one section of tree. We know little of dimensions above the level we are at because we all have to progress on to those, but if an example could be given of rising higher up the tree to find those levels, don't think it means elevation as such, because the tree is still the same one with all contained within it. That is the best way of perceiving it all, and this is why those of us willing to do so, can relate closely with those still in the physical. The difference is not location but vibration.

Q: Thank you, another good example. I have seen the term 'Summerlands' used to describe part of the spirit realms, is this where you have your home now?

A: Yes, I believe that is one name given to these levels. The etheric levels is another, differentiating them from the astral realms.

Q:I have read some odd things about this place, can you clarify it for us, from your perspective please?

A: There have been many differing theories written about these levels, including it being the realms of illusion. This isn't quite an accurate description. It is correct that things can be created by thought here, and travel is instant. It is also the levels where all things are possible and you can be, and have, all you want. This means if you wish to do things the longer way, through your own efforts, you can work in that way too. These levels reflect Earth and life on Earth without the negative side, there is no pain, no struggle to survive, no need to work for money, no illness. It is really an idealised

Earth. Here we gain understanding of how cause and effect operates and we also learn. It is possible to progress too in these levels but it takes a lot longer than incarnating because it is those negative aspects that teach us best. These levels though, are really more our home than Earth is, and it is here, that everyone travels to when sleeping. So which is the illusionary place, here, or Earth? Remember it is the physical body which breaks down and disintegrates whatever attempts are made to extend its duration.

Q: Thank you, that helps us understand better. Can we touch on a rather delicate matter now, that of emotional love. There is a belief that once we shed the physical, we shed all that goes with that, including any form of emotional relationships. Can you comment on that?

A: This is a tricky one because some are bound to be offended by the reply. However, clarification is essential because just as there are those who are quite happy to think they can be done with all that after passing, there will be just as many who are horrified by that notion. The first important fact is that there is no promiscuity here. I speak of my level because on some lower levels, where those on them haven't risen above such things, they find all that they seek in that direction, as well as other base desires. As I have tried to explain before, nobody is ever forced to go against their free will and if they still hanker after such things, until they learn differently, they are available. Please don't be shocked by that because all rise out of those so negative 'habits' eventually, and the fact they are allowed shows the benevolence and perfection of the Divine purpose.

I have spoken about group souls and the eternal relationship between true soul-mates. On these levels, that union is the only one sought or wanted. That love is emotional and every expression of it is possible, but it is far more beautiful than anything experienced on Earth. It is a total union in every way. And without emotional love, operating purely from unconditional love eventually creates detachment and isolation which was never the intention for us.

Q: Would it be possible for you to explain in the simplest terms, briefly about soul groups and soul-mates again please?

A: We are part of a soul group as you know, but you may not fully realise that during the early stages, as the souls break away to begin individual experiences, it doesn't all happen at once, but that break away is achieved in groups too. What eventually is left, is a certain number, say for instance, eighteen. But those will actually be nine pairs and will break away into pairs, just like all the others from the initial whole group, eventually becoming individuals but always having the strongest bond with the other half of that pair. However, there are also strong bonds to the other sixteen in the group, and bonds, though less strong, with all the others forming the entire soul group. These, all of them, are the bonds that last, the greatest of them being with the one forming the other half of your pairing. You will have experienced lives with that one many times, also though, lives without them, and with others, depending on what learning was required.

Some of those lives together would have been the other way round in gender to this lifetime, some where you were both the same gender, and through a whole range of different relationships. However, you eventually progress to a point where you can choose which gender you each prefer to be, and when you incarnate in those forms, probably several times, some lives together, some apart, that is usually the moment when you totally recognise each other as a pair when between lives here. Prior to that, you may not always recognise the extent of your bond together, but there is always a very strong attachment.

A similar state happens while in physical life too, it being well on in evolvement before you totally recognise each other. Throughout our times in between lives, we do usually meet up with others from our soul group, and many of these will have had links with us during the lifetime just finished. Equally others, including your greatest bond, may still be in physical life. This is why early spiritualist contacts from here say you meet up with your family, friends etc., again, but haven't then, had full knowledge of the soul groups and roles played. Now, it is all understood quite soon after returning here, at least at these levels.

Q: This is quite an advanced aspect of life after death, isn't it? I mean, we have such set ideas about relationships and all that here, but few people would imagine emotional relationships are possible there.

A: It has always been so but only now can it truly be accepted. There has been a lot of hypocrisy spoken in the name of religions; including the idea that sex is sinful and only for procreation, mankind's egoist misinterpretations of information given by those here. Fortunately these ideas are changing and the control they held is lessening now. That is what those ideas were all about, controlling the masses through fear. But it has resulted in a lot of warped thinking, and there are still those here who feel a reluctance in giving this information because so many are still caught up in that control cycle. Personally, I feel it is time to set matters straight.

Why should it be so different here, to life in the physical dimension? Some have a very strange idea of what is described as 'paradise'! Companionship is an essential for most on Earth, to give balance and quality to life. That doesn't alter with the shedding of the physical. The only things that are lost are the negative aspects, such as possessiveness, selfishness, lust, personal gratification. This is because we can see the role playing for karmic reasons created to highlight exactly those faults in us. That is why life and all in it, is so illusionary, but it has to be that way or we wouldn't achieve anything.

Q: Some may be quite shocked by all this, believing we all become angels drifting on clouds playing harps, or just sleep peacefully?

A: That just shows how controlling information has been. Also, because of the density and need for learning/experiences causing 'amnesia' of life here, it is very hard for those on Earth to think of themselves existing after death at all. It is too difficult to actually have any feeling of it. It is easier to picture being angels and resting in eternal peace, or even total oblivion - no need to worry about personal responsibility with that! But the dawning reality as you adjust to being in this dimension again, brings great joy once realisation takes over. At these levels, we have no real idea of what it is like in the higher realms but as we eventually reach them long after we finish incarnating, there has to be something even more wonderful than we have here.

The most important fact to remember is that nothing is ever forced on anyone. There is no judgment by others. The only one responsible for what you find here, is you. How you lived your life, what you chose to believe and so on. If your wish is to be alone here, then you will be. And if your belief is that you sleep between lives, then you will. But if your hope is for sharing everything joyfully with one special close companion you can love totally and emotionally, then that reality can be yours.

Q: Do awkward situations ever crop up? I mean supposing someone is happy with a soul-mate and then a former spouse or partner passes over believing in spending eternity together, as seems to be the general idea here?

A: This is rare but can happen although usually all is sorted out at the time of transition. Sometimes, if there is a stubbornly held possessiveness residue, then yes, awkward situations do happen. This is where guides are invaluable. They take over and help the person come to terms with the way things are. Mostly though, you find yourselves at different levels anyway and you will never be expected to be with anyone you don't wish to be, no matter what the physical relationship was.

Q: I was thinking how chaotic it could be for those, and there are many now, who have several marriages and/or serious relationships?

A: Exactly. That shows why we quickly learn about the role playing and karmic reasons for things. It is all very well worked out really. It wouldn't work any other way because there wouldn't be any movement or progress if all our previous physical relationships remained exactly as they were forever.

Q: Thinking about karma, what is the spiritual thinking on the subject of organ transplants?

A: This is quite an emotive subject on Earth, those who are adamantly for, and those equally adamantly against. There is no conflict in spiritual terms because what is meant to be will be. Those receiving transplants who subsequently die anyway, were meant to leave the physical then, just as those who die before a transplant becomes available.

By far the major consideration is with those who give, and receive, organs through transplants. Although apparently the identity of donors is usually kept from those receiving organs, in fact, they are known to each other on other levels and the whole procedure is agreed in advance, during sleep. There may be karmic reasons why someone agrees to depart and donate organs, or it may simply be a way out with dignity, in a way that gives to others allowing them opportunity to live on and fulfil some purpose. This also applies to children, on both sides. If this is hard to accept, just consider that it relates to another life when the 'child' was an adult personality.

However, it is very wrong for pressure to be exerted on those who have no wish or feeling to donate organs either for themselves, or departed loved ones. Where there is a shortage of organs to transplant, that is because all is as it should be. Equally, the most horrific 'advance' in spiritual terms, is developing the use of animals to provide transplants. Mankind has no idea what harm can ensue from this, or the karma attracted as a result. Mankind has abused this planet in ways that bring it close to destruction and he will damn himself further by abusing the souls of animals in that way. It is a serious error to regard animals as being there solely to benefit mankind. They are here to learn and evolve too, and are not capable of understanding agreement to provide organs at this stage of their progress. It is a mistake to cross species anyway as some are currently finding to their cost at the moment, and more examples of this will surface over the next few years, to show mankind he cannot assume the role of Supreme Creator. The need is to work with nature, not attempt to control it and to work with spirit in acceptance. The way forward in that respect, is in the creation of artificial replacements and these are the true advances because they carry no residues from the original owners.

Wherever a transplanted organ is successful, they carry effects. The receiver will change, the degree dependent on which organ is used. They will no longer be totally a sole entity but will, through agreement, carry traits of the original owner. There are reasons for this, far too many to explain simply, but all to do with karma and/or learning. The extent of these changes can be quite dramatic and distressing for those closest. They too have to accept the learning in that. Adjustments are required all round. There have been some documented accounts of some of the most severe changes brought about through receiving someone else's organs. But there are many more subtle ones which go unrecorded.

The important thing to remember in all matters relating to organ transplants is that there is no automatic 'right' for anyone to receive another's organ if their own is failing. Karmic/learning reasons for that failure and to attempt to control that by forcing others to donate, will perpetuate that experience, possibly into future lives. Universal law is absolute on that. There is no escape or avoidance, and only through agreement for a given purpose, can such things be resolved.

Q: Thank you, I am sure many will find that useful information. Geoff, could you explain a little about the various ways you communicate? It may help those who have experienced things they cannot explain.

A: I'll try although some aspects might be difficult to describe in terms of physical understanding. The non-tangible ways are mostly telepathic. When I speak to you, you hear me but mostly inwardly, telepathically. You see me via your third eye which carries an image directly into your mind. That is why you may be able to see and hear me, whereas someone walking by, would only see you, unless they were also psychic of course.

The important thing to remember is that we have a much higher vibration. This means what we say can be much faster than normal, and is why some direct channellers describe it as seeing images and having to interpret. Equally, some may 'see' a flash of something out of the corner of their eyes, and again, this is because of the vibrationary rate being much faster. It is not difficult but takes a conscious effort to slow that down sufficiently for those still in the physical dimension to be aware of, and that is why those who refuse to develop any degree of that awareness, deny all existence of the spiritual dimensions.

When it comes to materialising, allowing you to see with your physical eyes, that involves a different process. The first two are fairly simple and soon mastered by those willing to attempt contact. But anything more 'physical' requires much energy and the use of atoms and molecules from the physical dimension. Materialising requires us to lower our vibrations and densify our bodies which makes them appear, but rather like a shaped mist. There are ways for us to appear looking as physical as anyone still in that dimension, but it is quite a complex process to learn and practise. It is possible some of the people you see about are actually discarnate but have returned for some purpose, maybe something not completed or to give help somewhere. It isn't the process that is so skillful as being able to hold it for any length of time in the denser vibrations, and that takes practice.

A similar method is used to enable us to touch or move anything. But with this, we use a combination of atoms and thought. Remember the experiment we did in the summer where I demonstrated the difference using atoms and without? (J: Yes, there was a great difference. I hardly felt anything without the atoms. It was a bit like brushing up against a cobweb.) That is where thought alone is used and many people have probably experienced that at sometime, but by 'borrowing' atoms and molecules, when you held out your hand, you could actually feel my hand touching yours.

Q: Yes, there was no mistaking it. But I don't quite understand why the 'borrowed' atoms etc., don't retain their original form?

A: That is because nothing is actually solid. Everything around you is a collection of atoms held together by mass thought. Borrowing' a few from something makes only a slight difference to the object, but I can rearrange them to densify my own form.

Q: Does it take much effort?

A: It isn't effort in physical terms but more of a mental energy process. It has to be learned though, and practise helps. It is the only way we can interpenetrate the physical dimension without a physical body. It is also the way used by those here, to physically help where that is an option, and permitted.

Q: What about merging?

A: That really doesn't give much scope because all we do is become part of something else. It is really only used for observational purposes. That doesn't mean we are watching all the time, but sometimes it is necessary and that is one way of doing so. We can also merge with people for various purposes, as you know. Some may find that frightening, thinking of possession, but it cannot be attempted without permission and mutual agreement.

Q: What about ectoplasm?

A: Now that is something I know very little about. I understand it was an etheric material used a lot early in this century to demonstrate spiritual presence. But things do evolve here too, and we have moved on a pace beyond using that. The use of atoms and molecules gives us a denser and better result, actually allowing a degree of sharing more fully in physical life.

Q: Does electricity play any part?

A: Electricity is very easy to manipulate. It also provides a good example because it is invisible, yet see how much it can do. An understanding of electricity can give greater insight into what operating from spirit is like.

Q: Somehow we have an idea that once someone sheds the physical, they become all seeing, all knowing, can you cast some light on this aspect?

A: This goes back to the subject of beliefs again. I am not having a go at religious personnel, but really they do have a lot to answer for and it is because people seek better knowledge now, that the church' appeal is waning. Fault doesn't lie with the faith of course, but those given charge of it. Mortal men and women who interpret according to their own ideas, and this goes back a very long way, it gave the chance to control the masses by 'colouring' the truth. There is power in that, and some find it a very heady 'drug'. They all learn when they get over here.

This is why there is the notion once somebody dies they become akin to whatever idea of 'God' one has. Teaching gives us wondrous angels, and so they are, but we do not become angels ourselves as they follow a different evolutionary path, and we do not have their selfless total dedication or abilities. The expectation is misleading. True, we do have a wider perspective on things, and developed awareness helps, but we don't know it all, and our abilities are only slightly greater than when in physical life. We learn things, just the same as you do. But we don't get a magic wand to wave whenever something is requested. I am still very much me, with more awareness and having gained a little more knowledge - I hesitate to say wisdom - than I had before getting here. And it will still be a very long time before I aspire to the lofty heights of the highly evolved beings.

Q: Geoff, can you describe in a bit more detail, the dimension level where you are living now, and how it relates to this physical dimension please?

A: Certainly, spirit is a perfected state of physical life. There is no great change, either in personality, or in habitat, beyond an expansion not possible in the confines of the physical. This is because of the learning aspect of physical life, and the limitations of density. Here it is fairly static in as much as opportunities to progress take far longer than in the physical. To explain this further, look at physical life as a sort of condensed eternity. You have the beginning with birth. All is new and there is much to learn and experience. You move onto childhood, still learning, gaining. Young adulthood, with all its traumas and problems to work through. Adulthood, here you gain certain freedoms of choice and lifestyle. For the first time you can decide for yourself. This stage goes on for some time. Then you get to old age. Maturity. Much experience gained and respected. You have accumulated wisdom and knowledge. There is no need to go back to learning as a child, but you can still learn.

This example gives a clue to what life is like here, and why the links at this level are still strong to physical life. As we go from life to life, this has to be or we would be too far removed to fit into it so easily again. Only when we finish incarnating, having gained all that is necessary through experiencing physical life - that is, all necessary for us to evolve - can we think about moving into the higher/finer levels and leave physical life behind. Until that point, it all goes on much as before, each world reflecting the other.

Q: So life for you there, is still very much like life here?

A: Yes, given the choices I have made. In general there are differences of course, necessary ones. For instance, there is no reason for births in these dimensions, that is purely a method of bringing beings into physical life, a very efficient way too, which eases the spirit back into the denser life on earth. There is no need of that here. Returning here is more natural, and joyful. Literally just a stepping out, and stepping in.

There is no time structure so no clear cut day and night, seasons etc. And yet, paradoxically, we can still have those things if desired. There are astral levels where all these things are possible. There is no need to eat and drink to sustain our etheric bodies, but that is available too for as long as it is wanted, but nothing that harms or exploits another life, there are alternatives. We work at what we want to do, not out of need to pay the bills. And free will is still paramount, no-one interferes with that, or has any right to exert control over us.

Q: It seems a fairly perfect life, does it ever get boring?

A: How can it with so much to do and see? There are so many levels here, and no restrictions on visiting any of them. There are limitless things to do according to whatever pleases you. And there are pauses in it all when you return to Earth and take on another life - that too being your choice. There are countless work opportunities, and great socialising, none of it governed by time or other constraints. There are also marvellous and endless opportunities to study, learn; and for any hobby or anything you can think of. And, we can if we wish, take holidays for as long as we need, and where we wish to be. Only those who are most limited, could find it boring, and that is because they come here with such rigid beliefs which have to be released before they can truly experience all the wonders here.

Q: There are a lot of theories going around about a rise in consciousness on Earth, can you comment on that?

A: This is a vital jump in evolution. Things on Earth have degenerated into a dangerous state. The Earth is struggling to survive with all the rubbish dumped on, and in, it. The seas are dying, literally. Warnings have been ignored, people are too complacent. The old 'it won't happen to me' thinking is way out of date. It is happening, and it is happening now. That is why a shift is needed. There are a lot of ways being discussed but nothing is cast in concrete, yet. The population will be given every opportunity to do something themselves but time is not elastic on this. If necessary, certain drastic changes will be implemented. If people go on ignoring the state of things, and not caring, they will be shaken up. Earth is your physical home, if that dies, where will the human race live?

Q: I know from our conversations you always felt strongly about what was happening on this planet, is that why you have chosen to continue working in the same fields?

A: Yes, I felt I could be of some use, maybe more so from here. I was delighted to find I could continue doing the things I always enjoyed so much, and in fact, expand that to do things capable of making a real difference. It also meant I could stay in close touch with the Earth dimension which suits me too.

Q: I am sure many would be glad to hear that because some felt you went too soon, too young?

A: There isn't actually any such thing as too young, and maybe this gives me an opportunity to clear up another little inaccuracy - the belief that your length of life is determined before you incarnate. The muddle on this is because you take on certain purposes for your incarnation, and sometimes, there is a limit given for that. I won't go into the reasons as they are many and can be complicated. The thing to remember is, that as with everything else involving free will, you create your own life as it goes along. Sometimes this means a purpose has no chance of being completed or fulfilled. When that happens, at a certain point, we are offered the choice of continuing regardless, or of 'dying' so purposes can be fulfilled here, depending on the importance of them. This is done at subconscious level of course. So we can actually choose our moment of passing, choose to go when we want to. This is an important fact to grasp because it shows there are no victims, and also, that nothing 'out there' is controlling your life, only you do that.

It is slightly different with children. Often there, it is a life cut short for some reason previously, and just a few Earthly years required for some purpose. Sometimes it isn't even that, just a need to touch the Earth plane and then go back. But again, there are no victims. I realise that is hard to understand when dreadful events happen, but it is necessary to accept it. No-one can move on and live properly if they get themselves stuck in a victim mentality. It is a downward negative spiral. And purposes not achieved, still have to be done, even if it takes many lifetimes to do so. Personally I would like to see the word 'victim' vanquished totally from the language.

Q: Geoff, can you give any insight on why we are still mostly ignorant about the afterlife and spirit worlds? There doesn't seem to be much progress in terms of such knowledge breaking through the confusions, or actual proof, at least to satisfy the scientists.

A: Part of the problem lies in the way we think, based on things we are told. Our understanding of death, is of a soul going to some place 'not in this world'. That and other such repeated sayings give an element of detachment and separation which is false. The reason why there is not more contact and the whole spiritual side is so controversial, denied totally in many quarters, is because we have always been led to believe it is some distant world, far away and remote from us. But it isn't. The difference is not in world, but in vibration bringing a change in dimension, and if we can grasp that concept, it removes the barriers and opens the way for contact to flow.

We are so used to believing in only that which is visible to our physical eyes, that which we can touch and perceive as total 'reality'. Most people cannot even see their other, etheric selves, except in sleep and dream states. All that happens when we 'die', is that we shed the physical. What that means is whereas those who knew us could see us while physical, and accept us as 'here', from then on we can only be seen by the inner etheric eyes, outside of actual materialisations, but the world is the same and the spiritual dimension exists all around you, still living and being. It is not much different to electricity and other 'invisible' things you cannot see, but know are there.

For the most part, while incarnate, we dismiss the spiritual because of 'amnesia' and this idea of distance, so it seems less 'real' to us than what we can see physically. Once in spirit we can choose whether or not to 'see' the physical world all around, but even when we don't consciously tune into it, we are totally aware of its existence. It is never in doubt like those who deny the spirit 'worlds'

Let me give an example to demonstrate. A humming bird's wings move at such a fast rate, they become invisible unless filmed in slow motion. Observers see just a blur, a vibration. The body of the bird is still while its wings move, hovering to take its nourishment. This could be likened to a physical, incarnate being, standing next to someone now discarnate. The location is the same but the different vibration gives another dimension and because of it, both can exist in the same place. Psychics can see those discarnate beings in varying degrees depending on their development, to anyone else who hasn't yet developed those skills which all have, they are invisible. In the same way, higher, finer dimensions are invisible to us.

Q: This is something I have been asked about our nightly 'visits' into other dimensions during sleep state. If we all go into spirit each night, to learn, work, or whatever, why are there so many criminals and wrongdoers?

A: There are a number of reasons. Two things to bear in mind, first, those in the physical dimension, just as we here, can only go into the level attained. Until you progress, the levels above are too much for you in terms of vibration, energy, light etc. Many of those referred to in this question are lower down in progression terms, and while some of their 'visits' would be for learning, probably much of the time they would choose to go to various astral realms where they can just enjoy themselves. Secondly, all have free will and that can never be interfered with, so those who opt out of learning in favour of fun, can do so whenever they wish.

In some cases, crime is an addiction just as much as drink, drugs, cigarettes etc. Learning to overcome addictions is one of the big challenges of physical life. One that sadly is often not achieved requiring further periods of learning in lower spiritual realms, and sometimes, further lifetimes of dealing with addictions.

Such activities as crime, mostly come under negative control. Negative forces are attracted to physical degradations of all kinds, and can get a hold on those beings through them. The being is then encouraged to continue those activities and remain in that state to fuel the negative forces. What they do learn in spirit during sleep, remains submerged in the subconscious. Any attempt to surface it is over-ridden by free will and the compulsions of addiction.

However, the negative side is not without purpose, and in a lesser degree, is vital to our progression, This is because as we evolve, we need to achieve perfect balance and without one, you cannot fully appreciate the other. For example, without sorrow, how can you know the experience of joy? The problem now is how successful negative forces have become, constantly gaining strength from the weakness of the masses. And at the heart of that lies mankind's desire to control through fear, limitation and restriction. This is basically why a rise in vibration and consciousness is so essential at this time.

There is another, yet still linked, purpose for some criminals, and no doubt it will come as a surprise to know they are here to teach. The reasons are as multiple as personal paths to progress, but just to give an example - and remember it is always done by agreement and arrangement in sleep state - someone requires the experience of loss, letting go, being violated through theft; as part of their learning, or as part of karmic balancing. In that case, the criminal involved is actually giving service to that soul.

A trained observer can usually determine which is which. The addicted negative criminal is always mean, nasty and will produce various degrees of revulsion, sometimes also compassion, in higher evolved beings. Those who are here to teach will often be regarded as likable rogues, and it is those who can show remarkable examples of exercising a conscience too.

Q: I find all we have discussed most interesting and have no problems accepting even the most controversial details because somehow I know it is all correct and am comfortable with it all. But there may be those who are completely content with their lives and relationships who wouldn't want to think about it all being for the reasons given. Wouldn't they find it rather hard to accept and understand?

182

A: Possibly, but it doesn't really matter if some don't want to accept things, that is their choice. No-one can deny 'death', it is indisputable and a certainty all have to face at sometime; or deny that nothing physical lasts forever. That can be very comforting for those with 'bad' experiences. But I believe even those content with their lives, knowing it cannot be like that forever may well appreciate and value what they have more, and take better care of it all, including the environment around them because it all goes to making up the whole. Humans are very good at taking things for granted when all goes well, and that includes overlooking the needs of others not quite so fortunate. It does no harm drawing attention to the facts, and if that creates better understanding in some, leading to a sharing and caring beyond themselves, then there will be benefits all round. And any efforts in that direction are worthwhile.

Q: There is so much I want to know and could probably fill a book with questions alone but for now, a final question; Geoff, is there anything you want to say to sceptics and those who have other beliefs they insist are correct?

A: That is O.K. It is where they are at - the level they have reached. None of us is wrong. That way is their reality at the present time and therefore, is as true for them as our reality is for us. We are all learning and no-one has all the answers, yet. We are all seeking something to make sense of it all but far too often, when someone shares their own experiences, in a negative attempt to discredit, possibly out of fear, 'experts' are brought forward to comment. These have many wild and 'clutching at straws' theories such as it being 'imagination', or 'something to do with the brain'. But like everything else, theories are all they are, they cannot be adequately proven any more than the top religious leaders can prove all they preach. So it brings it back to the personal responsibility we each have to make up our own minds. Read it all, then accept only what feels right, that which suits you personally and feels quite comfortable. Don't think you have to accept everything just because it is in print, however respected. Reject anything that causes you fear. There is nothing to fear. Once you make up your own mind on it, focus on that, and it is that which will be your reality when the time comes for you to leave the physical dimension. But do accept that others have different beliefs and respect that as being where they are at. Do so with love, and without judgment. And just remember, we all get there eventually, that is one fact you can be sure of, so it might as well be the way you want it to be.

# Afterword

Recently an elderly man died in our village. A lovely man also a millionaire with no surviving family. His home was full of beautiful antiques and a few days after he passed over, even before the funeral, the empty house was burgled. This unpleasant act will bring its own karmic results on the perpetrators. The following day, a flurry of activity re-secured the house with new alarms and other measures to protect the remaining antiques, material possessions no longer required by their owner.

In other parts of our world fires rage out of control, destroying further, the planet's lungs. There are devastating earthquakes some caused by nuclear tests in other areas. And there is famine - we see scenes of tiny children looking wizened and old before their time, skeletal forms and bewildered tear-stained faces. And people who never complain but just sit and wait to die, with incredible dignity. Could these people be suffering in an attempt to rouse mass compassion and caring, necessary elements for the new age?

This is a world of extremes. Some, relatively few, have so much. The top twenty or thirty wealthiest people have bank balances of obscene amounts, more than one home - some have several, and all manner of material possessions. On the other side, a vast majority of people have little or nothing. When there is so much available among the few, why are there still homeless people; starving people? There is no spirituality in amassing money and possessions. What use are those things when so much has to be done to protect them, and the owners worry constantly about them being stolen?

We all need to find a better system for living, one that honours and respects all life, not just humans. There was never a greater need to bring forward our spiritual side and begin creating a world that truly reflects the love, caring and compassion of the Creator; rather than the more often seen, arrogant egoism of mankind. Only then can we truly have pride in our spirituality, and be worthy of our continuance through eternity.

This book was suggested, instigated, and guided throughout by Geoff, and although it was jointly created between us both, I feel it is only right that the final words in it should be his:

# Geoff's Afterword

I appreciate that some of the material in this book may be hard to swallow after so many centuries of limited thinking. Yet even over those centuries things have changed enormously, evolved, progressed and moved on. This is the clue to the Universe and life, including that beyond death. Nothing stays the same. All of creation is constantly moving forward, developing, growing. As it does so on Earth, it begins beyond, and without those constant changes, that movement, there would be no Universe.

If this book helps to open minds and hearts just a little, starting a thought process that eventually brings an awakening towards the meaning of it all, an understanding of what physical life is all about, then I will consider this possibly my greatest work. And yet the work I did in my recent physical life, in a sense, opened the way for this book and the knowledge it attempts to convey.

Perhaps that life was my 'school room', my training ground of preparation, and the purpose for it. I offer that for consideration, so you can look at your lives and begin to see the greater Divine purpose running through them all. And if this book makes its mark in heralding that necessary change in consciousness, then we, its authors, will have given a great service to mankind, and my happiness will be complete.

G.H.1998

# P.A.W.S.

## The Pets and Wildlife Sanctuary
Patron: Jilly Cooper
Chairman: Paul Kennedy   Reg'd Charity No. 1014125

P.A.W.S. animal sanctuary is run on mainly spiritual ideals, treating all animals with respect as valid equal co-habitants of our planet. We always use healing and alternative treatments alongside conventional veterinary care. (We also offer absent healing for any life form in need)

Some permanent residents among our animal family

We receive no state aid. Donations always welcome.
P.A.W.S., 2 Marine Cottages, Coat, Somerset, TA12 6AR.
Tel 01935 824848, email pawsmartock@hotmail.com,
website: http://beehive.thisissomerset.co.uk/paws

# Some other titles published by Capall Bann:

## Reflections From Beyond    Jeannie H. Judd plus channelling Geoff Hamilton

This second book , sequel to *Beyond the Rainbow Cloud,* continues the account of a remarkable contact between the spiritual and physical dimensions. Everything moves on, in the etheric world too, Geoff Hamilton's great love of plants has led him to study them there in much greater depth, producing surprising results that can benefit our physical lives if we follow his gardening suggestions in part one. In part two, further knowledge is channelled through Jeannie including Geoff's valid concerns about physical issues causing more harm to our planet, and why we need to urgently halt the damage and restore the true natural balance of the Earth. Geoff also demonstrates his skill as a teller of entertaining significant tales. ISBN 186163 147 2

## The Other Kingdoms Speak - What the Animals, Plants, Crystals, Extraterrestrials, Angels, Mermaids & Fairies Have to Say
Helena Hawley

*"Helena's efforts inspire and uplift us in every chapter...leaves the reader feeling lighter and brighter as a spiritual quality shines out from the pages....I am sure many readers will find something of value in these books"* Jeannie H. Judd.    This is a book of communications from the spiritual dimensions. The diversity of themes covered includes the "Council of Animals", other animals, tree consciousness, mermaids, fairies, angels and interaction with extraterrestrials with wisdom and learning from past lives. The need to recreate the balance of the planet is explained, but more than this, our true place in the scheme of things, part of the whole, no longer needing to be apart from it. The other species on many levels of existence all offer us their loving help and energy in making a great leap forward in human development. The energies of wisdom and love are extended to the reader through the medium of both words and inspired artwork, including full colour plates. ISBN 1 898307 062X        £10.95

## Gardening For Wildlife    Ron Wilson

**"If you have only one wildlife book, this is the one to have. The information contained in this book is invaluable. A very interesting read for young and old alike, to which you will always refer." The Professional Gardener**    *"..a real delight...a fascinating read...all of the methods I have tried so far have gleaned superb results"* Touchstone    *"lively, colloquial style...quick and easy to read...inspiring and full of helpful tips'* Place
*"..a nice book...lively drawings which clearly illustrate techniques...covers everything...a good starter book"* Permaculture
A few 'modifications' and additions could enhance the value of most gardens for wildlife. That is what this book is all about. It offers practical advice and ideas for improvements and where possible suggests the inclusion of 'extra' features which will support and encourage a rich diversity of plant, insect, bird and animal life. Plants, foods and features are all described in plain English. Everything in this book is explained in straightforward terms to enable anyone to help their local wildlife. ISBN 1 86163 011 5    £10.95

# FREE DETAILED CATALOGUE

Capall Bann is owned and run by people actively involved in many of the areas in which we publish. A detailed illustrated catalogue is available on request, SAE or International Postal Coupon appreciated. **Titles can be ordered direct from Capall Bann, post free in the UK** (cheque or PO with order) or from good bookshops and specialist outlets.

Do contact us for details on the latest releases at: **Capall Bann Publishing, Auton Farm, Milverton, Somerset TA4 1NE.** Titles include:

Arthur - The Legend Unveiled, C Johnson & E Lung
Auguries and Omens - The Magical Lore of Birds, Yvonne Aburrow
Between Earth and Sky, Julia Day
Caer Sidhe - Celtic Astrology and Astronomy, Vol 1, Michael Bayley
Cat's Company, Ann Walker
Celtic Faery Shamanism, Catrin James
Celtic Lore & Druidic Ritual, Rhiannon Ryall
Celtic Saints and the Glastonbury Zodiac, Mary Caine
Crystal Clear - A Guide to Quartz Crystal, Jennifer Dent
Crystal Doorways, Simon & Sue Lilly
Crossing the Borderlines - Guising, Masking & Ritual Animal Disguise in the
        European Tradition, Nigel Pennick
Dragons of the West, Nigel Pennick
Eildon Tree (The) Romany Language & Lore, Michael Hoadley
Enchanted Forest - The Magical Lore of Trees, Yvonne Aburrow
Eternally Yours Faithfully, Roy Radford & Evelyn Gregory
Everything You Always Wanted To Know About Your Body, But So Far
        Nobody's Been Able To Tell You, Chris Thomas & D Baker
Fairies in the Irish Tradition, Molly Gowen
From Past to Future Life, Dr Roger Webber
Gardening For Wildlife Ron Wilson
Handbook For Pagan Healers, Liz Joan
Handbook of Fairies, Ronan Coghlan
Healing Book, The, Chris Thomas and Diane Baker
Healing Homes, Jennifer Dent
Healing Journeys, Paul Williamson
Healing Stones, Sue Philips
Herb Craft - Shamanic & Ritual Use of Herbs, Lavender & Franklin
Legend of Robin Hood, The, Richard Rutherford-Moore
Lore of the Sacred Horse, Marion Davies
Magic of Herbs - A Complete Home Herbal, Rhiannon Ryall

Magical Guardians - Exploring the Spirit and Nature of Trees, Philip Heselton
Magical History of the Horse, Janet Farrar & Virginia Russell
Magical Lore of Animals, Yvonne Aburrow
Magical Lore of Cats, Marion Davies
Magical Lore of Herbs, Marion Davies
Magick Without Peers, Ariadne Rainbird & David Rankine
Mind Massage - 60 Creative Visualisations, Marlene Maundrill
Mystic Life of Animals, Ann Walker
New Celtic Oracle The, Nigel Pennick & Nigel Jackson
Pagan Feasts - Seasonal Food for the 8 Festivals, Franklin & Phillips
Patchwork of Magic - Living in a Pagan World, Julia Day
Pathworking - A Practical Book of Guided Meditations, Pete Jennings
Personal Power, Anna Franklin
Places of Pilgrimage and Healing, Adrian Cooper
Practical Meditation, Steve Hounsome
Psychic Self Defence - Real Solutions, Jan Brodie
Real Fairies, David Tame
Reality - How It Works & Why It Mostly Doesn't, Rik Dent
Romany Tapestry, Michael Houghton
Sacred Animals, Gordon MacLellan
Sacred Celtic Animals, Marion Davies, Ill. Simon Rouse
Sacred Dorset - On the Path of the Dragon, Peter Knight
Sacred Grove - The Mysteries of the Forest, Yvonne Aburrow
Sacred Geometry, Nigel Pennick
Sacred Nature, Ancient Wisdom & Modern Meanings, A Cooper
Sacred Ring - Pagan Origins of British Folk Festivals, M. Howard
Seasonal Magic - Diary of a Village Witch, Paddy Slade
Self Enlightenment, Mayan O'Brien
Spirits of the Air, Jaq D Hawkins
Subterranean Kingdom, The, revised 2nd ed, Nigel Pennick
Symbols of Ancient Gods, Rhiannon Ryall
Talking to the Earth, Gordon MacLellan
Tree: Essence of Healing, Simon & Sue Lilly
Wildwood King , Philip Kane
Wondrous Land - The Faery Faith of Ireland by Dr Kay Mullin
Your Talking Pet, Ann Walker

# FREE detailed catalogue and FREE 'Inspiration' magazine

## Contact: Capall Bann Publishing, Auton Farm, Milverton, Somerset, TA4 1NE